And the Incorrect Answer Is: "No Comment"

Ron Palmer & Mike McCarthy

1st Edition - © 2005

And The Incorrect Answer Is: "No Comment"

© Ron Palmer, CPP & Mike McCarthy

For Information - Contact:

The Palmer/McCarthy Group, LLC
5147 S. Harvard Ave. #163
Tulsa, OK 74135
www.mediacrisisgurus.com

ISBN: 1-59872-057-0

Contents

FOREWORD

"As a Sigma Delta Chi Award Winning Journalist, Best Selling Author, and Magazine Publisher myself, this book is powerfully crafted to empower you to take the high ground and convert any media interaction (whether positive or negative) into an interaction you will later look back upon and be proud of.

In today's media world where ugly appears to be journalists' desire, YOU must recognize that the media is not there to tell your story, they are there, in fact, to tell their story . . . this book empowers you with the strategies and tactics to non-confrontationally re-gain the high ground of honor, integrity, dignity, and create perceptions of goodness in the eyes and ears of the public (or whom ever your constituents may be)!

As a Certified Management Consultant, I am afforded the honor of working with Fortune 100 companies, major Associations, and Government Agencies up to the Director and Secretary level - "No Comment" truly is a death nail in an media interview - whether radio, television, newspaper, magazine, journal, blog, or web based medium. The Point-Counter Point of this book is great, explosive and gives you perspectives from both sides of the "microphone" and when you are in that rare of rare situations to be graced by a "professional journalist" the quality of that outcome will always be fair and balanced.

Until then, you can't afford to be ill prepared for the unexpected ambush interview, crises responses situation, or routine media inquiry . . . this book is your field book to success . . . every member of your organization that does or may remotely be placed into a situation of dealing with the media should have a copy of this book at their finger tips

Jeffrey L. Magee, Ph.D., PDM, CSP, CMC

Founder: Jeff Magee International   Publisher: *Performance Magazine*
www.JeffreyMagee.com   www.ThePerformanceMagazine.com

Toll free 1-877-90-MAGEE
MANAGERIAL- LEADERSHIP & SALES TRAINING WITHOUT LIMITS!

What They're Saying:

"This should be required reading for anyone who might ever come close to the media. It can make things easier for people on both sides of the fence. I've seen dozens of people make terrible mistakes on camera, because they were under pressure and trying to improvise. This information can be insurance against that kind of disaster. It's far better to be knowledgeable and prepared than clueless and panicked . . . I've read a number articles and PR papers on the subject, and yours is the best I've seen. It has the good the bad and the ugly."

Charles Ely
KTUL News, Channel 8, News Anchor - Tulsa Oklahoma

As I read through the guidelines established in this text, I suddenly realized that this was not theory, but practiced, proven principles . . . the standards and techniques presented by the authors will help you deal with the media, not just from your head, but from the place where real confidence and understanding reside - your heart.

Reverend Danny Lynchard
Director, Tulsa, Ok. Police and Fire Chaplaincy Corps

The book, "And the Incorrect Answer is, 'No Comment' ", is an extremely astute and concise analysis of the current state of media operations in the United States. The book offers valuable suggestions for executives and media spokespersons of any organization on how to deal effectively with the various representatives of the media during either daily or crises situations. I would strongly recommend it be read by anyone who deals with the media on a regular basis.

Edward J. Tully
Retired Chief, Education and Communications Arts Unit, FBI Academy
Former Executive Director, Major Cities Chiefs of Police Association

And. . .

The Media Crisis Gurus realize there are readers who will find errors in our text. We don't do this intentionally, but know they may exist despite our best efforts. We include them in the final draft so as to please all of you those who take great pleasure in looking for or finding these. We know we are not perfect and take great satisfaction in that fact. Regarding any errors, we have "No Comment." - The Media Crisis Gurus

vi

PART ONE:

You Too

Can Be a

Media Spokesperson

Chapter 1

WHO SHOULD READ THIS BOOK?

There is no easy answer to this question. A starting point in figuring out why you should read further can be guided by several benchmarks:

- Do I own a company?
- Do I have employees?
- Am I a supervisor, middle manager, or executive?
- Is my line of work controversial?
- Do I work in the field of government, education, petroleum products, chemical products, public utilities, or other critical infrastructure service providers?
- Am I responsible for facility maintenance?
- Does my work relate to safety and security issues?
- Can a natural disaster (flood, tornado, hurricane, or winter storm) affect my building or operations?
- Is terrorism or sabotage a consideration of my work place?

If your answer to any of these questions is "yes" then you need to proceed because you could easily become a "target" of a media interview, especially if something goes wrong. But what could go wrong?

You only need to go as far as your daily newspaper, TV/ Radio nightly (or continuous) news coverage to determine what can go wrong. Read or listen carefully to what constitutes a news story today and you will readily find where danger lurks. Anything and everything happens. It's reported, re-reported, dissected, discussed, and cussed. Every detail, every mistake, and most every indiscretion becomes fodder that day for the news reporter.

Most of us believe that the sensational things we read in the paper and hear on our television sets won't or can't happen to us. These things happen in other places and to other people who, mostly, can't seem to adequately explain the why or how of what happened, what they are doing to stop what is happening, or have a clue how they will recover in the aftermath.

The reality of a workplace or school violence incident has been played out many times on our television screens and newspapers in recent years. Chemical spills, power outages, sabotage, and terrorism also have become prominent news items and are now routinely reported. No geographic region is immune from the touch of Mother Nature and the destruction she can deal in the form of violent, destructive, and deadly weather. Internal
2

malfeasance, fraud, and theft also find their way to the papers, the screen, and on the Internet.

Moreover, the age of instant news surrounds us. We no longer have the luxury of a "slow" or non-existent media response to a crisis situation.

Reach into your pocket, purse, desk, or backpack and you will likely find a cell phone. Yours may have a built-in camera. What that means is instant, live-stream video news reporting whether a reporter is on-scene or not. You now must be prepared to deal with media issues instantly or be swept away in a rush of media coverage that can ruin your professional reputation, your organization's image, and adversely affect your market share (private) or your funding (public).

What this means to you in considering reading further is simply this:

- You can choose not to look foolish when the reporters come calling by developing a basic set of media skills.
- You can look like a seasoned media veteran.
- You have the opportunity to learn how to develop a company media message that will serve you well in all media interviews.

- A poor media performance may mean the end of your career and stymie your business growth–the <u>bottom line</u> of why this book is important to your professional development.

To collect your free gift, worth $75, send an email to: <u>info@mediacrisisgurus.com</u>

Chapter 2

THE FORMAT: POINT/COUNTERPOINT

The reason it takes two guys to write this book is they each provide very differing perspectives on the successful media relations equation. Neither perspective is particularly academic in nature. Both authors have learned from real life experience. The format of the book reflects and emphasizes this practical experience, rather than dwelling on the academic side of "Media Relations 101" as promoted by some other authors professing the expertise, but perhaps lacking the actual exposure in the media and the public scrutiny that exposure brings.

As differing perspectives bring differing ideas to the same subject, the book is presented in various chapters pointing to the general theme that "No Comment" is indeed the incorrect answer. However, to better express the sometimes differing opinions of the authors, a **Point/Counterpoint** format is used for each chapter and the subsections within those chapters. It's a verbal boxing match on some issues. On others it becomes a mutual admiration society of agreement that the points being made <u>are</u> the ways that will allow you to succeed when confronted with the inevitable crisis media interview, press conference, or non-crisis inquiry.

THE POINT

As former Chief of Police of the Portsmouth, Virginia and Tulsa, Oklahoma Police Departments, Ron Palmer has been interviewed hundreds of times during his 31-year career in law enforcement. He currently owns and is CEO of Palmer Security Consulting (on the web at: www.palmersecurityconsulting.com.) His POINT sections are generally more pragmatic in nature, drawing upon lessons learned while acting as a spokesperson in cases involving primarily natural disasters, manmade disasters, significant death and/or injury, or public policy matters.

Being the interviewee in a time of crisis or even a seemingly "vanilla" news story is a far more dangerous position to be in than that of asking the questions. That is not to say that the POINT view is always adversarial in nature. Experience teaches one to be wary of the media and perhaps distrusting of the stated agenda at times. However, understanding the media agenda can, in fact, be used to your advantage if you know how to do so.

6

THE COUNTERPOINT

At the outset of any type of media interview, the news reporter has the upper hand. They may know more about the subject than you think they might know. They certainly know what questions will be asked and where they plan to "lead" the interviewee. To carry the analogy of a boxing match a little further, the momentum of any interview can be handed to or earned by either participant at any time. It's all about preparation, what you know about technique, and the context of the verbal sparring that goes on during most investigative interviews.

Mike McCarthy takes his tenured skills as a radio and television reporter/personality and turns them into the COUNTERPOINT sections in response to the POINT. He draws on over 30 years experience in a variety of radio and television markets and has logged thousands of interviews during his career. He owns a media/marketing consulting firm, Mike McCarthy and Associates, that specializes in product promotion and image building. He is skilled in assessing, stalking, and "bagging" government officials, rock stars, movie and TV stars, and other prominent personalities while working in Tulsa, Birmingham, Charlotte, Baton Rouge, and Oklahoma City.

Providing the insider media guy information in the COUNTERPOINTS, the reader now has it all:

- A look from both sides of the microphone.
- Differing perspectives applicable to a variety of venues.
- Agreement and disagreement on what's right and wrong.
- The combined media experience of over 60 years.
- A one-two punch on how to avoid "No Comment" and come out a winner.

To collect your free gift, worth $75, send an email to: info@mediacrisisgurus.com

Chapter 3

INSTANT NEWS AND CRISIS MANAGEMENT

In an age of "instant news" reporting, the media's propensity to use that capability in a crisis, emergency, or disaster is a "given" for all reporters and photojournalists (big word for cameraperson) in the field. The drill for them is this: Be there. Be there first. Get the "story" on the air as soon as possible so the reporter can claim on camera that this is "breaking" or "exclusive" footage. Scooping the other media outlets for a story in a crisis situation is considered good 21st century journalism.

Obviously, if you or your business is having the crisis or emergency on any given day, the intrusion of the media is an undesirable but inevitable distraction. With today's technology, you must understand video or photographic images will be generated immediately. You must also understand that in any crisis/emergency event a reporter will immediately begin seeking a story about:

- What went wrong?
- Whose responsibility / fault is it?
- How could this have ever happened?

- Are there deaths or injuries? How many? Why?
- When will the death/destruction/carnage, etc. cease?
- What are your recovery plans?
- How do you plan to fix it—now, tomorrow, the future?

Notice that "<u>a</u>" is highlighted above. "<u>A</u>" story is all they want and need. This is what they are assigned to do today. Tomorrow is a clean slate for new stories. Whether they get the <u>correct</u> story or actually any part of the truth about the event is up to you and how you prepare yourself for that moment. <u>Your</u> story and <u>a</u> story may be entirely different animals. Your goal as a person who may be responsible for the facility/operation or acting as a spokesperson is to assure that <u>your</u> story is the one that "airs" or is written up in your local paper.

This book is about knowing how to prepare. You should walk away with some new, immediately applicable, practical skills and knowledge that will allow you to survive the media onslaught in times of crisis. Moreover, if you apply the book's concepts you will likely sound smarter, give them <u>the</u> story you want them to have, and appreciate the need to never say, "NO COMMENT"!

PART TWO:

Who, What, When, Where, Why, and How?

Chapter 4

WHO CONDUCTS AND GIVES MEDIA INTERVIEWS?

If you have a position of responsibility in a corporate, education, or government venue you may be called upon to give a media interview in times of crisis. During non-crisis times/events your company may appoint someone to be the spokesperson for media inquires, or the boss will do that. In a large organization there may be designated Public Information personnel that speak for the organization as a matter of routine.

Think a moment about your current work situation. Could an emergency situation rapidly develop at your work place? If you think you are immune from an emergency/crisis, you are not seeing the big picture and your beliefs are not based in fact. The news is literally filled with crisis events every day.

Mistakenly, people believe it will just not happen in their back yard and certainly not at the perceived safe haven of a workplace. Today we may be lucky that it didn't happen to us, but it is happening to someone right now as you read this sentence. To better prepare you must understand the types of crisis you may be dealing with.

There are three general types of crisis:
- <u>Natural</u> - flood, tornado, hurricane, winter storm
- <u>Internal man-made</u> - fire, sabotage, workplace violence, industrial accident, Hazmat leak, embezzlement, etc.
- <u>External man-made</u> - acts of terrorism, certain crimes (robbery, armed assaults, and arson to name a few.)

Even though you think it can't happen at your workplace, the potential for crisis is, in fact, always present and will happen when you least expect them. If this crisis event takes place during your watch and the spokespersons are not available or have been killed or injured, someone must step up to give the company's story. That person may be you. ARE YOU READY TO TAKE ON THAT CHALLENGE AND RESPONSIBILITY?

Depending on your position and stature in your company, you may not be called upon to provide "official statements" to the media in times of non-crisis. The vanilla, good-news, touchy-feely story will be handled by those designated to do that duty. But in times of crisis, all bets are off and it is a whole new ball game. <u>Anyone</u> - yes, anyone - can be thrown into the breach of becoming the media spokesperson in a crisis. If that role falls at your doorstep one day, you can be prepared with some simple preparation and thought, even though it may not be in your job description.

Conversely, those working in all media venues (print, TV, radio) are paid to talk and fill page space or air time. Let there be no mistakes; they are paid to probe, prompt, pry, cajole, sweet talk, investigate, and shame people just like you into talking to them. Their goal at the end of the day is to tell their bosses that they got a story. (Please note: not necessarily **the correct** story.)

The term "journalist," although still used by the old guard of newspaper columnists, has generally fallen by the wayside in favor of the more popular and recognizable term, "reporter." More than likely a reporter may have a descriptive adjective thrown in front of their name which gives them stature or identification in their field such as: investigative, health, senior, junior, embedded, police, business, safety, etc. Likely, you won't be dealing with "correspondents."

Oftentimes, depending on the size of the media market, a reporter may hold several "titles." In some smaller media markets, a field reporter (the person that talks to you) can also be an anchor (the person that sits at the desk on your nightly news.) Newspaper, TV, and radio reporters all generally report to a news editor, news director, or the like. These editors are the bosses and they make daily determinations as to what will appear on your television screen, radio news, and the newspapers.

Equally important for you to understand is that at the beginning of the day there is extensive discussion at each media outlet as to what stories will be covered. The news assignment editor/director determines what stories will be "chased" on a slow news day and makes those assignments. When there is a prominent, ongoing story lasting several days, that story may be reexamined until the editors feel they are beating a dead horse. Then, they finally move on.

When an emergency, disaster, or crisis occurs within the listening or circulation area of an individual media market, all plans for the day are discarded and a full frontal assault is made on the incident.

On-duty reporters are sent, live coverage trucks and helicopters are dispatched, and off-duty reporters may be called back to create "seamless" coverage. If an incident rises to this level, then you, as a media spokesperson, are at a disadvantage, as each individual reporter will be seeking a story - any story relating to the incident. If your story is picked up on the "wire" you may also be looking at national/international coverage. So how important do you think it is to be prepared?

The saving grace for any spokesperson in an emergency situation is to hope that the emergency occurs in the dark of night or on a weekend. Media outlets downsize for these periods and will not likely send a reporter or crews unless you are in an extremely large media market. But be ready to brace yourself for the onslaught of media inquiries at first light in the morning.

Reporters are folks just like you. They have families, obligations, mortgages, car payments, etc. Many will have some type of journalism or communications degree. When you start out reporting you are poorly paid. The better you get (meaning the better/more sensational stories you find) the better you get paid or you are rewarded by moving on to larger media markets. Thus, reporters are looking for "meaty" stories that shorten the ladder to success and more money. They look at you, your company, and the chinks in your armor to accomplish their goals.

Although it may seem so at first blush, the media/corporate relationship need not be adversarial. There exists the opportunity to build relationships with reporters that do not seek the investigative reporting Pulitzer Prize. Those that will write or report fairly (more than just one side) are out there and should be cultivated as allies in times of non-crisis so you have credit to write the checks you need when times of crisis do come your way. Wooing the media is not entirely an accurate description, but it should be and will be considered as you move forward.

To collect your free gift, worth $75, send an email to: info@mediacrisisgurus.com

---

Chapter 5

UNDER WHAT CIRCUMSTANCES ARE MEDIA INTERVIEWS GIVEN?

In this day and age of advanced technology, any circumstance, at any location, can generate a media interview. We have all seen the embedded reporter in a war zone broadcasting broken transmissions via a cell phone. No light? Not a problem! Low light, infrared, and other new technologies allow us as spokespersons to grant an interview any time - if we want to.

"If we want to" is the key element to your success. On rare occasion, you as a spokesperson will not have the opportunity to pick and choose the time and location of your interview. The more aggressive reporters will seek you out and try to get comments before a situation actually stabilizes. This means you may be granting an interview before you know the facts, before the injured or dead are treated and removed, or before the fire is out or Hazmat cloud has cleared.

Avoid this situation to the best of your ability. It is not in anyone's best interest to give an interview unprepared with a backdrop of your company's building burning, children running from a school in terror, or the ambulances lining up to take away the injured. This does not generally work. What may be said in the heat of an emergency may prove to be inaccurate, inflammatory, and/or create a basis for litigation or adversely impact your corporate image.

The more prudent course of action is to preplan the crisis media event at least to the extent that you have picked possible backdrops for media interviews and know where you are going to "stage" the reporters, their equipment, and vehicles. You must also preplan to the extent of designating who will be speaking and have an alternate spokesperson if the principal person is unavailable at the time of the emergency.

It is not in your best interest to be too eager to get the story out if you are unsure exactly what the story may be. The reporter's urgency in getting a story to their audience as quickly as possible and beating the competition is obvious. You should not buy into this media induced panic. A story just for the sake of a story to get the media off your back will generally result in an incomplete story that may be riddled with inaccurate information.

Choose a time early on in the crisis to give your first interview - **after** you have verified, factual information.

Attempt to have "home field" advantage by conducting the interview in comfortable surroundings (as comfortable as they can be for you). Assemble all media representatives at once so that your message is consistent. You will better control what is being said and have witnesses to what you did say so there will be commonality of story line for all media outlets. Avoid exclusives, private interviews, and favoritism. In addition, be sure to avoid a "No Comment" posture or attitude. Something must be said. That something should be the preface to your overall message and the corporate theme you want to promote.

In a crisis situation that is developing or is lengthy thinking that one interview alone will be enough is simply underestimating the situation and not realistic. Updating the media representatives at predetermined locations and set times is necessary if the story plays out over several hours or days. If you can foresee how the event may play out, then each media interview you give should preface the next. Much like a well-scripted play, there are beginnings, middles, and endings to crisis events no matter how chaotic they might appear.

Your first interview sets the stage. What you know now provides the material for this segment of the event. As the event is played out, there may be more breaking news events that deserve comment but generally you will move into a stabilization stage that plays off of the triggering event and usually relates to the initial incident. Lastly, both you and the reporters covering the story will sense that the story is coming to an end. At this point, you have a golden opportunity to capitalize on the good things that have been done and how you plan to make things better in the future. You have more time to craft the message and should be less rushed in its delivery. Your ending should be better than your beginning, but it all should be themed.

To collect your free gift, worth $75, send an email to: info@mediacrisisgurus.com

Chapter 6

WHEN MAY YOU HAVE TO GIVE A MEDIA INTERVIEW?

"When" is related to the concepts covered under **"What Circumstances"** do you give an interview.   In crisis situations, it is important that you do not speak to the media too early in the event. The pressure to do so may be great, but you should be the one choosing the **"when"** rather than being manipulated by the reporter. Giving an interview too early can create the following adverse situations for you.

- Misstatement of fact or lack of complete knowledge of the scope of the incident.
- Lack of empathy for those affected by the event (victims, families, first responders, customers, etc.)
- Create the need for wholesale corrections later. Better to have waited a few minutes for verified fact than to speak while uninformed or confused about the status of the situation.
- Forming the basis of future litigation, product liability, or decreased market share as a result of "knee jerk" statements.

22

You may think that there is never a good time for the "when." The media sharks are circling. The situation has yet to fully stabilize. You feel the pressure to say something, but you feel unprepared to do so. For you as a spokesperson the moment of truth has come. It is indeed a fragile moment that none of us cares to be in, but it is evident that something must be said. The bloody goat is in the water (that would be you), and the sharks (that would be the reporters) are circling for the kill.

How do you know that the time is right? Is now, "when?" The inexperienced spokesperson may not know at all. They may fear the inevitable or commit the sin of uttering the "no comment" comment. With the skills learned in this book, some planning, and a dose of good common sense, you actually know when it is time to step up to the microphone and be interviewed for the first time in a crisis situation.

Some guidelines that may assist you in determining when to grant this first interview include:

- The immediate danger posed/revealed in the initial incident has passed, been contained, and no continuing or heightened threat is perceived.
- First responders have ruled out the possibility of secondary devices (in the case of explosion).

- Individuals requiring immediate medical attention that can be readily reached have received treatment on scene or have been removed to medical facilities.
- Unaccounted for personnel have been located in some manner, affected personnel cared for, and families notified.
- You have accurate assessments of damage and assurances of containment of the event.
- You have reasonably accurate counts of injured or dead and where they are being removed to and/or treated.

Other indicators of the "when" to give that first interview may be driven by the media representatives responding to the event. For example:

- If the reporters are seeking stories elsewhere because of your delay in responding to inquires or scheduling a timely interview, you need to give a statement immediately (i.e. they are talking to the uninformed, competitors, disgruntled employees, or neighbors, etc.)
- If you continue to deny live coverage to TV and radio in perceived defiance to their news deadlines and news programming times, the reporters will go ahead and create a story absent your message.

- You sense exasperation in being denied access to a spokesperson - which would be **you**. If they aren't getting the initial comments of substance from you within the first half-hour, a story line will be started with or without you. Your message beyond this point may not support the already developed story for the day.

You are able to buy some time with the media by giving a brief, factual message early on about the status of the incident with the promise of more information to follow at a predetermined time and place. If you need or choose to use this tactic, be sure you make good on what you promise without fail. It's good business to begin with and creates good will with the media representatives the next time you face them.

In non-crisis situations you have more control of interview scheduling, but you still must keep in mind media deadline times if you want to build sound, long-lasting, pay-off relationships with your local media outlets. They'll recognize that you understand them, appreciate them, and will probably be more forgiving of going after the bloody goat in the water when it becomes feeding time again.

Chapter 7

WHERE IS THE MEAT OF A NEWS STORY?

There is a media adage that speaks to the sensationalism of a story and the press coverage that is afforded that event. **"If it bleeds, it leads"** is, in our experience, an accurate description of how much air time or how many column inches of a newspaper are devoted to covering the story.

One might mistakenly believe that this adage pertains literally only to events where bloodshed has occurred: drive-by shootings, homicide, mass fatalities, bombings, etc. For the most part, this rings true, but the bleeding doesn't necessarily stop at the level of real blood being let.

Examples of corporate blood letting include stock fraud, insider trading scandals, embezzlement, product failure, chemical release, workplace violence issue, or other internal malfeasance that become known to the public. These types of corporate "meltdowns" are abundantly evident.

Exxon faced this type of corporate exposure with tons of oil spilled in the Valdez incident. Firestone drastically reduced their market share of tire sales and adversely impacted a well established corporate image as they struggled with the media inquiries relating to the Ford Explorer roll-overs. Enron failed both in the boardroom and in subsequent press conferences relating to the internal fraud found to be rampant. And who would have guessed that Martha Stewart would be sentenced to Federal prison?

Despite best efforts, no person, organization, or entity is immune from media exposure. Throw in the mix the unanticipated attacks by outsiders via crimes/acts of terrorism directed toward the company or employees, or Mother Nature's wrath, and the meat of any news story can be generated without warning. Bleeding still leads, but the bleeding takes on a new "face" of corporate chaos, disintegration, or failure.

The reporter, by virtue of his/her training, job description, and seemingly endless inquisitive nature, usually will look past what you may be telling him to get to the "dirt". This propensity seems to be especially evident if the reporter believes that you are not being truthful, or perceives (or is told) that there is more to the story than what is evident at first blush.

So the "meat" of any news story surrounding a crisis event usually centers on the sensationalism of the event itself. You can almost count on the following being reported in any news story covering a crisis (not necessarily in this order):

- **Death** - "Body Count" <u>will</u> be reported.
- **Serious Injury/Other Injury** - "Body Count" again. Also important is where they are being treated, which can generate "spin-off" stories of human interest or negatives from the disgruntled.
- **How Did This Happen? What Caused the Incident?**
- **Who is Responsible?**
- **How Will They Be Held Accountable?**
- **What Are You or Your Company Doing For the Victims and Their Families?**
- **Will the Victims Be Compensated?**
- **When Will Things Be Back To Normal?** - Strikes at the heart of a good recovery plan, if you have one.

In an ongoing crisis, the "meat" of the story reported for that hour, day, week, month, or year might change as time moves to the right. The initial factual reports of death and injury are finalized and usually put to rest early on in the reporting sequence. Then, the good reporter will focus on the "how", "why" and "who" using the facts of death and injury to support further inquires of those who will bear the responsibility for the loss or devastation.

One of the authors observed firsthand how the meat of a story can readily change from the concept of **"If it bleeds, it leads"** to that of where to place responsibility for those deaths and injuries as the situation stabilizes and moves toward recovery.

On July 17, 1981, the citizens of Kansas City, Missouri endured one of the most tragic moments in the city's history. On that evening, the Hyatt Regency Hotel "Tea Dance" was being held in the hotel lobby. This weekly event had become extremely popular, attended by hundreds of people enjoying the surroundings of the relatively new hotel and the live band that was provided for the patrons.

The hotel and hotel lobby were both upscale. One of the featured architectural pieces in the multi-story lobby was two "skywalks" that linked one side of the over 100 foot long lobby to the other on the upper floors. The skywalks, located directly above the dance floor, afforded an unobstructed view of the lobby below and, on this night, the opportunity to enjoy the live music and festivities on both the dance floor and in the lobby.

The skywalks, because of their vantage point, became crowded with dozens of people on each level. Accounts of what happened vary, but most are in agreement that the people were using the large skywalks as both a preferred observation point and as an additional dancing venue above the designated dance floor on the lobby floor. As the music played, the uppermost skywalk (4th floor) began to sway, came loose from its underpinnings, fell onto the 2nd floor skywalk and its patrons, then onto the lobby below. Literally, hundreds of tons of concrete and steel from the two skywalks came crashing down on unsuspecting partygoers.

Instant chaos followed. Some were trapped alive. Some were instantly killed and entombed in the steel that, just minutes before, was their dance floor. Many of those lucky enough to avoid the massive pieces of concrete and steel as they fell saw loved ones, friends, and neighbors crushed by the force of the impact. 114 people died that evening and in the days that followed. Hundreds of others were seriously injured and removed to local hospitals. Many were disfigured or permanently disabled. By some miracle, some walked away without a scrape other than the horrible mental picture of what they had witnessed.

The magnitude of this news story is not likely one you would face. With some degree of certainty you would assume that none of the hotel staff on duty that day or any of the Hyatt corporate officials could have anticipated what happened. These things don't happen in new structures. Yet it did. And yes, they had to talk about it, just as you might have to talk about your event.

The after-the-fact observation of the news reporting of the Hyatt incident is provided to you from the eyes of the initial responding Uniformed Police Captain dispatched to the hotel and one of your co-authors. This brief chronological observation of events is not accurate to the day and hour, but it does give the reader an idea of how time changes the "meat" or focus of the story in an enduring event like the Hyatt.

- **Time of Incident (TOI)** - TV news crews are already covering the Tea Dance. Actual footage of the event and aftermath is recorded - edited tape is shown on the nightly news.
- **TOI through 2nd Hour** - The news media have unlimited access to the site. First aid, search, recovery, and rescue efforts hamper the efforts to establish of an effective outer perimeter to control access. The focus of the reporters is on the carnage and the number of dead and injured.

- **Hour 3 through Day 1** - The outer and inner perimeter and command post are established. A media staging site is established, but proves to be insufficient as the magnitude of event is fully realized. National and international news coverage takes shape. The media focus is still primarily on the dead and injured and the continuation of rescue efforts. Some human interest aspects and hints of assessing blame start to emerge in the stories. Other stories evolve relating to the survivors, witnesses, and first responders.

- **Day 1 through Week 1** - The rescue efforts continue for three days (24-7) before all the skywalk debris and the remaining dead are removed. There are a few belated good news rescue stories of survivors trapped somewhere underneath the twisted steel. Media reporters continue to be denied access to the site. The site commander finally grants guided tours to selected media representatives and continues with updates - albeit less frequently. News stories now focus on:
    1. The aftermath and recovery
    2. Human Interest
    3. The owner's and architects response
    4. The investigation into the cause
    5. Victim and survivor sympathy
    6. Remedies to avoid future like tragedies

- **Week 1 through Month 6** – The designing architects are brought into the media briefings held by hotel management. The skywalks will not be incorporated in the new hotel lobby design upon reopening. Stories shift to determining the cause, reporting on additional deaths and recovery of victims, and now, the anticipated litigation.

- **Month 6 - Year 10+** – The Hyatt Hotel reopens with a newly designed lobby. The millions of dollars paid out in litigation settlements are routinely reported. Both the hotel and architect are ultimately held responsible. Stories are still numerous but move toward the "who", "what", "why", and litigation aspects and away from the human aspects of the event. The original death and destruction stories fall by the wayside acting only as a backdrop for the justification of the on-going litigation.

- **2001 - 20 Year Anniversary** – The Hyatt Hotel disaster of 1981 is remembered in a national television news documentary commemorating the 20 year anniversary. Stories of individuals who were there and their acts of heroism are resurrected from old media files and film footage. What was said by the responding spokespersons in 1981 plays out as the recorded media history of this most tragic event. The point is: Media statements made today, shape history tomorrow.

As you can see from the preceding real situation, assessing blame to someone or some entity is a popular reporting methodology. Understandably, no one wants to accept this responsibility. But, in some circumstances, standing up and accepting responsibility for an event can turn out to be a positive for your organization.

For example, Johnson and Johnson took an unprecedented bold step in removing all Tylenol products from the shelves when it was discovered that some Tylenol products had been tainted with poison by an outside source, causing customers to fall ill or die. Johnson and Johnson stood up and quickly announced both the problem and their response. They went beyond what might have been expected by removing all Tylenol products from the marketplace until the poison issue was resolved in the minds of both their customers and the reporters covering the situation.

In the short term, accepting responsibility created a tremendous loss of market share for one of their most popular pain relief products. The corporate strategy, as it appears many years after the incident, was to assure both their name and product image remained intact. Though Johnson and Johnson took a huge hit initially, their strategy paid off handsomely later as Tylenol was "reintroduced" in new, safer, tamper-proof packaging (leading the industry is such packaging) and actually taking a bigger bite of market share than before the incident.

These examples illustrate the meat of the story can be, and should be, an integral part of the corporate message you craft and deliver to the media in times of crisis. "No Comment" was never an option for Johnson & Johnson but it appears that it was for Firestone, Exxon, and others in similar situations. You be the judge of who came out a winner.

To collect your free gift, worth $75, send an email to: info@mediacrisisgurus.com

Chapter 8

HOW CAN YOU BENEFIT OR SUFFER FROM MEDIA EXPOSURE?

We have already seen examples in which corporations or individuals have suffered or benefited from media exposure. Every day we informally evaluate whether a particular interview was beneficial or detrimental to the participants. As observers of media behavior, the authors are perhaps more aware of "good" or "bad" interviews and what benefit may be derived. But we all evaluate the interviews we see, hear, and read. How many times have we thought that a particular interviewee appears to be nervous, unprepared, or just plain stupid? Conversely, we have seen individuals that are prepared, extremely well versed in the subject and, most importantly, able to convey a message that effectively promotes themselves and their organization.

"Benefit" and "suffering" are relative terms when observing the overall effectiveness of a media interview. You benefit if your message and interview cast you and your organization in a favorable light. Believe it or not, this can be done in both non-crisis and crisis situations. We have seen, and will continue to see, examples of the poor unfortunate soul selected to be the spokesperson for his company in a crisis who comes away from the experience with accolades from his boss, his peers, and the public for the way they "handled" it. Crisis or not, you can not only survive, you can thrive.

In **non-crisis situations**, the media can routinely benefit your organization/company if you successful in relaying the good news stories to them. This is usually accomplished through the public information or public relations staff or designated spokesperson. If your organization is not of the size to support such a position, these duties should fall to a designated individual with some basic training - similar to what is offered within these pages. In a **crisis situation,** for a small company, you may not have the benefit of cultivating media relationships beforehand. But even the smallest of companies can make that effort if you so chose.

That being said it does require some effort to get good news stories about your company in the paper or on television. What better place to look for favorable news reporting in times of **non-crisis** than the business editor of your local paper. As stated previously, the reporter's job is to fill copy or air time. If you can routinely provide "good news" press releases about the operations of your company and the great things you are doing either in the workplace or community, you build credit with those news agencies for the times when the news might not be so good.

At a minimum, the media folk will know your name, know a little about what your organization does, and the successes you have had. The cultivation of media relationships is perhaps easier and may be more important in the world of non-profits. From the reporter's perspective, a business owner or representative who tries to initiate a "relationship" or sends a good news story to a reporter or editor may just be trying to get free advertising, circumventing the advertising folks. In essence, you are looking for free publicity (in part, at least), and the reporter may be suspect of this "evil" ploy on your part.

On the other hand, a "not-for-profit" has no apparent profit motive but does want to promote itself for the good things it does to enhance fund raising or to get more people involved with their cause. The reporter is less suspicious of this (for whatever reason) and may run with a "good news" story more readily than they would for a profit entity.

Where "non-profits" often fail is not taking the time to make calls to the media outlets, following up on those, and not understanding the media agenda of primarily filling space and air time. "Good news" is obviously not aired or run

38

with the same fervor as sensationalism, but it can get you **free** (emphasis on free), favorable publicity if you include it as part of your marketing strategy.

The "suffering" that can be incurred by a media spokesperson or organization is most evident in an interview that goes bad - heads south as they say. The reporter may sense this "suffering" from the outset of the interview, and may, if so inclined, go directly to the throat for the kill. It is similar to the belief that dogs can sense fear in humans. So it seems that reporters can sense the ill-prepared, the liar, the prevaricator, the cover-up, and the buffoon. They smile and start with the softball questions that later set up the "I'm going to rip your heart out" question. We like to couch this phenomenon in our *"Managing the Media in Times of Crisis"* seminars as *"Crisis Communication Rules to Die By"* (see next page). Thus, the suffering ceases and you literally die on the vine right there in the interview, in your boss' office later or worse yet, in the court of public opinion.

Later we'll explore how to stop or preclude the suffering and let you survive and thrive. If, however, you have a tendency to look at the dark side and like the beating you may take at the hands of the media, here are:

8 Communication Rules to Die By:

1. Speculate

2. Overstate, Understate, Or Showboat

3. Hold A Press Conference Without Preparing

4. Respond To Hostile Questions In A Hostile Manner

5. Blame Others For Your Own Mistakes

6. Reveal Confidential Information

7. Show Favoritism or Give Exclusives To Particular Media Outlet or Reporter

8. Talk Off The Record

Looking for the ultimate **"kiss of death"** - read on!

To collect your free gift, worth $75, send an email to: info@mediacrisisgurus.com

---

Chapter 9

WHY COMMENTING IS NECESSARY!

The title of this book strongly suggests that "No Comment" is indeed the incorrect answer when responding to media questions. We have already reinforced that thought several times. But why is it so inappropriate? We would argue, with much agreement from other media "experts", that "no comment" is really a strong, poignant, comment. In fact, if you examine more closely the underpinnings of the "no comment" comment, you find that it may be the most damning, self-indicting thing you can say.

How many times have you watched television, listened to the radio, or read a newspaper or news magazine and seen "no comment" as the response to the really tough question(s) of the interview? What do you think at this point? You can pretty much outline that thought process by these questions that you likely ask yourself:

- Are they hiding or concealing something I should know?
- Are they saying "no comment" because they don't want to incriminate themselves, others, or their company?
- Are they lying?

- What conditions or events prevent them from commenting to a legitimate question tied to the news story?
- Why, at this point, does this person choose to be evasive?
- Are these folks or their company crooks?

You likely log that "no comment" in your memory with the notation that this person or this person's organization is up to something because they **chose** not to be forthright. Down the road your memory may be jogged with this less than favorable first impression and you decide to:

- Watch their actions or the company further.
- Follow up on this statement and watch the news further to see if other "no-comments" follow (reinforcing your initial negative thoughts.)
- Not vote for them.
- Not buy their product.
- Hope they go to jail.
- Not invest in their company.
- Not like this person and what they stand for.

If the lay person is put off or is suspicious of a "no comment" response then just imagine what a reporter thinks. The reporter is trained to respond to "no comment" with a far greater degree of skepticism and distrust than the lay person. They do not appreciate the person dodging the question. Remember, they are trying to fill column inches in a newspaper or record a sound/video bite for their newscast, so a "no comment" response means they can only fill that "air" or "space" with speculation.

The "no comment" response may be aired as given or the reporter may chastise you in their own way with a more sarcastic, "And Mr. Doe refused to answer this reporter's questions regarding XYZ, stating they had "no comment" relating to the *(insert the important event or crisis they are reporting)*. More to follow on these developments as station XYZ investigates further." WHOA! Where did anyone mention an investigation? Moreover, why did my "no comment" response lead to this?

No matter how innocent or off-hand you are in uttering "no comment", the reporter and the public in general will not allow you the benefit of that innocence. You have created doubt in your honesty and perhaps thrown up a shroud of concealment which challenges the reporter to overcome. The "why" of you not commenting will become the story beyond or behind the story and may actually be pursued several days past the time when the crisis or non-crisis event ends. You have painted yourself into a corner of public doubt which will require some skill to extricate if you are pursued by a zealous reporter or editor that senses the bloody goat in the water.

The sharks will not just swim toward the blood. They may go directly for the jugular (your jugular) in this situation because you have, in polite language, made them very angry. There are, of course, other terms for anger that they will utter under their breath about you, what you are doing, and how they plan to even the score with you because you could not even answer the simplest of their questions without being a wise guy and telling them "no comment". Moreover, it is likely that they will win, as you do not own the television/radio station or keep 55-gallon drums of ink in your warehouse that allows you to print newspapers.

Let's examine more closely the damage that might be done with a demonstration of what could occur after that fateful encounter with "No Comment":

- Jane Smith, reporter for XYZ news asks a legitimate question regarding the report she is trying to file on the crisis situation in which you now find yourself.
- You find the question one that may be disturbing, one you haven't prepared for, or one that you find may put blame upon you or your organization.
- You search your soul and knowledge base for an answer that touches the question in any manner

whatsoever and all that you can generate in your own mind is: "Oh my God, I can't answer that!"

- Then in a moment of great solemn sincerity, the truth as you know it to be (at least at this moment) tumbles from your lips and you recite the only words that you can muster, "I have no comment on that matter."

- God forbid if you do the "no comment" deed in a press conference. If you did, you have not only shown your true self to Ms. Smith but you have now perked the interest of every reporter, in every media venue, and in an age of instant news coverage shown that:
    - ✓ You are being evasive, deceptive, and suspicious.
    - ✓ You know something but will not share it.
    - ✓ You don't know anything—why waste our time?

- Ms. Smith will likely ask the question again just to clarify your stupidity and to see if you might have misunderstood the simple question that she asked.

- You may reiterate your stupidity by answering again "No comment," or you may have sufficiently regained your senses to bring a more enlightened perspective to the question. (Ref: The Guru's CD *"What Do You Say, When You Can't Say Anything?"*)

- In any event, the damage has been done. You have become a sacrificial lamb (or goat) for this moment of news reporting.

- The interview (or press conference) being over, Ms. Smith, XYZ news reporter, will likely not report your "no comment" story as "the" story, but you may see your sorry face on the screen or your lack of inspirational words immortalized in the paper that afternoon or the next morning. You may be a part of the story but you won't be "the" story.

- You will go back to your office and think you out-foxed the media by not commenting, not realizing the damage you have caused because you had no message and you were unprepared to deal with the questions posed to you. You live to fight another day with "no comment" as the only arrow in your quiver.

WAIT! This is not the end to our "No Comment" news interview. Ms. Smith and her peers leave your office or press conference location still looking for a ("the") story. Why? Because you have given them nothing with which to fill their page or airtime. Why? Because you failed to understand how to best use the media to your advantage and craft a story that could have enhanced your organization's image, no matter how bad the situation.

Ms. Smith departs (with some degree of frustration and perhaps anger) to find the story to do her job for that day. As you have not made her job easy, she now has to find a story that looks not only at the incident at hand but at the added dimension of why the company spokesperson does not want to talk about it. (And why is that, Mr./Ms. Spokesperson? Do you know?) Ms. Smith is now on a hunt for opinions from those who do not have your best interests at heart, including your competitors, disgruntled employees, uninformed witnesses, and the families of those dead or injured. The reality is that she is seeking anybody that will talk to her about the incident since you won't.

You might say, "So what?" If you do, think about that response for a moment. It may be more damaging to the overall perception of you and your organization than the original "no comment". At this point, you cannot sufficiently recover from the "no comment" act to create a message, agenda, story, or any other favorable press coverage that will save you from the initial blunder of "no comment."

You've lost this one. If there is a second chance then you may get the opportunity to do better the next time. Like first impressions, you don't often get a second chance to make a favorable one. "No Comment" can and will hurt you. Moreover, if you choose to take that same posture again and again with the media, the higher the level of distrust the media will have of you and your organization.

Corporate attorneys and legal counsel will often advise that you can't get "hurt" with "No Comment". In this sense, "hurt" means saying something now that will result in an indefensible position in litigation later. But many attorneys, while obviously litigation savvy, are not as conscious as they should be regarding the impact of such statements made on corporate image, market share, and the reputations of their spokespersons on the firing line.

People expect attorneys to say "No Comment" because of what they do, who they are, and/or the restrictions placed upon them by the court. But the public does not expect (nor deserve) those outside the legal profession to use this crutch of poor public relations to speak to situations that have impact and implications for others in the community beyond the walls of the corporate headquarters.

"No Comment" is indeed a comment (or commentary) and may be the worst of the worst of what to say when cornered. In the world of reporting, a reporter worth calling himself that will understand and tolerate those who have mastered the art of saying something while saying nothing at all. This too may be distasteful but you've got to respect (a little at least) that this person has attempted to get past the multiple issues surrounding the "No Comment" response and on to something that will satisfy the reporter's need to get "a" story for the day.

That is the reporter's job. Commenting, even by saying something that says nothing, gets you past the initial hurdle of the distrust, suspicion, and reputation that a "No Comment" will bring to you. Keep reading for techniques on how to say something when you believe you can't say anything.

Chapter 10

THE 10 COMMANDMENTS OF A WINNING MEDIA STRATEGY

Looking for the right word to describe the favorable relationship you want to develop for your organization with local media representatives is difficult. We sometimes use the word "woo", but please not in a romantic sense. You should not attempt to make love to or court the media, as Mr. Webster defines "woo" in his latest "unabridged" version. The media will usually not return your affection in kind and you will end up feeling hurt and used. Perhaps no love lost?

However, "woo" or "wooing" in the sense that one would want to "endeavor to gain favor of" or "make a favorable impression with" does carry the correct connotation. The media can be courted, prompted, or convinced of certain facts that allow you to develop a cordial relationship. Again, this is usually done in the context of a non-crisis situation. It's hard to woo, let alone like, the media folks in a crisis.

Note: We do not go as far as to say "trusting relationship." That may come if you develop a lot of media contact over the long term. Stronger relationships of trust can then be formed. Be tentative and wary, and never fully trust the media relationships you may develop. This is a telling, yet unfortunate, indictment on the state of universal media relations.

Usually, the best you can hope for is building credibility with the media in times of non-crisis so that you have deposits in your account when you start cashing checks (so to speak) on that relationship in times of crisis. This could be better defined as a "Winning Media Strategy." If done correctly and with some diligence, this becomes your best defense and offense in dealing in either a crisis or non-crisis media event.

The remainder of the book is devoted to developing a "Winning Media Strategy" with real life experiences of the POINT/COUNTERPOINT format - an experienced reporter and one of their interview "victims." Our mission is to assist you in getting past "No Comment" to something more substantive for your media encounters.

The chapters in **Part Three** of this text take the basics of our "Winning Media Strategy" and permanently etch them into stone. The Media Crisis Gurus take you on a behind the scenes, down and dirty, lessons learned, search for the truth of what the media wants from you and how you can best provide it. Coming down from the media mount, we bring you:

The 10 Commandments of a Winning Media Strategy

1. Understand the Media Agenda
2. Don't Create Obstacles
3. Do Your Homework
4. Understand the Differences Between Print, Radio, and TV
5. Stay Cool - Be Professional
6. Get Over It
7. Craft Your Own Media Message
8. Tell the Truth
9. Strive to Thrive, Not Just Survive
10. Avoid "No Comment"

As you continue your journey to a better understanding of how to get past "No Comment" and build a new, improved skill set for media and press relations, keep an open mind, keep your sights set on the future, and know that you can succeed in any media encounter if you take to heart our practical advice.

PART THREE:

Insider Scoop that

Makes You a

Winner

Chapter 11

UNDERSTANDING THE MEDIA AGENDA

POINT:

It would be too easy for the POINT version of "Understanding the Media Agenda" to be simply stated as: "An agenda? Most reporters don't have a clue much less an agenda!" This discussion could end with that thought alone for those shallow thinkers who believe they will find, or currently know, the right formula for beating media representatives at their own game.

The media agenda has, in part, been previously stated in simplistic terms as "getting a story." To put the agenda in very understandable terms, you could conclude it is nothing more than this:

1. Reporters are hired at a nominal wage to do several nominal tasks - write, read, interview, make short presentations on TV or radio, and last, but not least, do what the bosses (editors/news directors) tell them to do.

2. Reporters go to work with mostly an empty slate for the news day unless they have been assigned a continuing news story or are working on a special assignment. They are assigned the day's work tasks much like you and I are assigned work in our jobs.

3. Much like our jobs as well, the tasks that are assigned at the beginning of the day may change as the day progresses, depending upon what becomes "newsworthy." Perhaps their task for the day could be directed at you or your company when crisis strikes.

4. Many less tenured reporters don't yet understand that they can look for news beyond what is assigned to them. They remain content with filling the slate, as both marching and fighting all pay the same.

5. So, John/Jane Doe reporter shows up for work, figuratively punches the clock, heads off to the reporter/editor meeting, assignments are made to go get the news. Then the reporters all go their separate ways to get a story on the topic assigned to them.

6. They return several hours later with a story in hand to meet the deadline for that day. Without crisis there is little overtime for media types.

7. JOB DONE! And that my friend is the media agenda. Simply put – no big deal – it's a wrap for the day.

8. The following day they repeat the same steps again, IF there is no crisis.

But what is news without crisis? Most of the people I know in the news business would call a day without crisis a very bad news day. Now that seems a little contradictory, but it is absolutely true. Media outlets do not survive by being the outlet known for their fluffy puppy dog, feel good, mom, apple pie, and the American flag reporting. They survive (read: ratings or share of market) if the dog has drowned or been tortured, you have deep depression, mom has been missing for days, the apple pie is tainted with anthrax, and the flag is being burned.

Thus, on beyond the basics of filling the page or the air time, the agenda reeks of havoc, investigative reporting, finding "dirty laundry", and making sure that your crisis is covered with the tag line of "breaking news", or better yet, "an exclusive". The overall agenda is not as simplistic as you might initially think.

Yet there are caveats and intricacies of the media agenda that are readily recognizable if you often have occasion to deal with the reporters. Most of us don't have that luxury to sort all this out after giving 10, 25, 50, or a 100+ interviews. Unlike some government entities, most corporations will not have the media scrutiny/exposure that promotes an individual or a staff of "public information" personnel to fully understand the day-in, day-out, ever changing media agenda. One of the purposes of this book is to give you a better understanding of this without the exposure and the trial, and (more often) the accompanying errors.

From the perspective of someone who has given more media interviews than they can remember – the interviewee point of view, as it were, here are some common themes to look for as you read between the lines of the basic media agenda of filling "column inches" or air time:

- Remember the axiom "what bleeds, leads." Your good news story will likely be shelved if a crisis news story is generated the same day or same week. Conversely, if you are the crisis, the media agenda will be to look at you, your event, and/or your organization with a microscope until the media is satisfied that they have sucked it dry or there is another crisis event to take its place.

- Each crisis story has many facets: factual, human interest, finger pointing, etc. Know that you may be expected to respond to any and all of these facets during an interview or follow-up to your news conference or release. Think through the possibilities of the agendas that may surround your particular story or event.

- Don't be fooled or lulled into a false sense of security that the reporter you are talking to is your own personal version of "Dumb and Dumber". Thinking that the reporter doesn't know the difference between "come here" and "sic 'em" will turn on you in a heartbeat. There is a real agenda hiding behind every reporter's dumber than a box of rocks approach, looks, and questions. It's the old "rope-a-dope," with you being the dope. Reporters know exactly what they are doing - reeling in the catch of the day when you bite at the bait.

- The media agenda for an ambitious reporter trying to get a promotion, raise, transfer to a bigger market, Pulitzer Prize in journalism, etc. will be, in a few extreme cases, a stop-at-nothing approach to get the story, the exclusive, the photos, the video, and all that goes with it at the expense of their own integrity, morals, and ethics. If they are not concerned with their own integrity, they will not be concerned with yours or the integrity of your organization. Even a novice spokesperson can spot these folks. Give them facts but do not attempt to befriend them in an attempt to defuse their ambition - it will not happen. They will be unscrupulous today and they will be unscrupulous tomorrow, the next day, the day after that, and perhaps the rest of their professional lives.

- In all media venues (print, radio, TV) there are some very hardworking news reporters who go beyond the stereotypical description of just doing their job. These folks are easy to spot as well. They possess the intelligence, drive, desire, **AND** ethics that make them a pleasure to work with in even the worst of situations. They are characterized by a sense of fairness, unbiased reporting, an appreciation for the history of any given event, and value the sanctity of human suffering and loss. They ask the tough questions without the arrogance or contempt that may be evident in their less tenured peers. They become the true craftsmen/yeomen in their trade. They can sometimes be the toughest of interviewers but you will feel you were given a fair shake in the aftermath.

Seek out these individuals in times of crisis. They will listen to your message, they will seek the truth, and moreover, they will share your pain for the loss you may have experienced your crisis. Best of all, they will likely be media representatives that you can trust in both good and bad times. Sound, two-sided relationships can be developed with this type of reporter.

So, the media agenda is what? It is often a moving target, guided by the day or a particular moment in time. But be aware that the moving target may be you. If it is, then you have the responsibility to respond as a professional. When you have the skills and know the turf you are playing on, there is no home field advantage for the reporter. It is a neutral site, the playing field is level, and the bull's-eye that has been painted on you by the media, just got a whole lot smaller.

The one thing you can't do with any degree of success is to expect to avoid the numerous agendas by the all too common serpentine diversion of saying "NO COMMENT."

COUNTERPOINT:

Oh, waah, waah, waah and boo-hoo. The big bad media is picking on you again. We're out to get you. We want to make you look bad, hold you accountable for your actions, expose your dirty laundry, hold you up to public scrutiny, show the world what you've swept under the rug and you don't like it.

GET OVER IT!

We exist in the same reality you do. We are what we are and we ain't goin' away.

DEAL WITH IT!

Ron, you are right, "If it bleeds it leads." Why? Not because we are a bunch of evil ghouls and sickos, but because that's what the public not only wants but demands. They want "news" not fluff. And how do we know what the people want? They tell us every day, through ratings and circulation numbers, research, and bottom line - bucks, dollars, and revenue generation.

You can analyze the media's agenda "till the cows come home," but the overriding factor is simple - PROFIT.

Why are the New York Times and Washington Post perceived as "liberal" and the Chicago Tribune considered "conservative?" Part of it is history and tradition - original owners who set the editorial direction. But these newspaper giants would not have survived and thrived had they not given their customers what they wanted. The long-term direction of any successful media outlet is predicated on keeping the customer satisfied.

Fox News is an excellent example of the media's number one agenda: making a profit. Many today proclaim Fox owner, Rupert Murdock, either the new messiah or the devil incarnate based on how they perceive Fox News. Liberals hate it. Conservatives can't get enough of it. Most people could care less. Murdock is a conservative, so you would expect his media outlets to reflect his views. But Murdock's first major US TV venture was Fox TV which features programming aimed and focused at young, urban "blue state" viewers. Why? Because that's where the need was - the hole, the niche - the most potential revenue source.

Fox TV super-served a specific target audience that was not being well served by the Big Three networks. The decision to program "The Simpson's," "In Living Color," "Tracy Ullman," and "Married With Children" to appeal to young urban Americans was strategic. Hit 'em where they ain't. This is the classic flanker move in guerilla marketing. Fox reached critical mass in their target, consolidated and then added the NFL and Major League Baseball to expand the brand, a frontal assault on the Big Three networks.

Had Fox TV reflected the personality of its owner they certainly wouldn't have programmed "The Simpson's." And they probably would have gone the way of The Dupont Network.

Fox News comes MUCH closer to reflecting Murdock's politics than Fox TV, but not BECAUSE of his politics. The Fox News programming slant has everything to do with filling a need. Fox TV is targeted to conservative, suburban, 25-54 year old, white males simply because nobody else was serving that audience effectively. Find a need and fill it is Marketing 101, and filling the need is what Fox did to remarkable success. Fox discovered a disaffected group, played on that disaffection, and gave that group what they wanted. Raw meat for "red staters" and a ratings / revenue success story.

The point of this example is that the media's agenda has little to do with liberal versus conservative, despite the popular misconception, and everything to do with profits. Try not to get bogged down with the popular perception that the media is this monolithic, evil entity that's out to get you. It's not true. We're just after the story. All that anger and indignation you may feel about us is simply counter-productive. Don't take it personally. Realize that we do what we do for the same reason you do what you do - to make a buck. Once you've internalized that, we can move on to what directly affects you. The media's secondary agenda - filling the space/time - getting a story that keeps those ratings, circulation, and revenue numbers up there.

.

The sensational sells. Sizzle sells. Pathos, crisis, violence, conflagration sells. Eagle scouts and bake sales - not so much.

So if your inevitable crisis sizzles, you are "A" story. Maybe "THE" story. But don't feel doomed just yet. How you portray the crisis and how you handle the media will go a long way in determining the length and intensity of the coverage and whether your crisis is "A" story versus "THE" story. How YOU manage us during your crisis could very well determine how well and IF you and your organization survive the crisis.

Acquiring a working knowledge of your local media is vital to your long-term survival as a spokesperson for your organization and for the organization itself. At some point in your organizational career you will have to deal with us. Without the tools to effectively deal with us or, if you choose to ignore and fear us, you could be S.O.L. when the crisis occurs.

To be effective in virtually any business context you must build relationships, network, and do your homework. It's the same with us media types. Take the time to do a thorough analysis of your local media and get to know some of the major players whether they are managers, anchors, reporters, or personalities. Do the same kind of "schmooze" you would do with any other major client. Then when the crisis hits you'll be prepared to be successful.

Countless surveys tell us the number one fear of Americans is the fear of speaking in public. Shoving a camera or a microphone in your face just exacerbates that fear. Let's face it; those of us who speak in public for a living are regarded by most folks with a mixture of admiration, awe, envy, and resentment. Because my job is to be there reporting the crisis or disaster and because I have to ask the hard questions, it's no wonder media people are at the top in both "Most" and "Least" admired profession surveys. But if you can face your fears, you can conquer them. That's the first step to effectively managing the media in a crisis.

There are a number of important steps in the process. The crisis media plan is a top priority and we will get more specific on how you develop yours later in this book. For now, visualize those in your organization that you think will be most effective in dealing with the media. It should be a short list. Everyone else in the organization refers media inquiries to this select and, soon to be, well-trained group.

Those on the list will become your media advisory committee. It will be the committee's charge, by utilizing "the six degrees of separation," to target a "player" in the local media community. You'll want to target someone who is familiar with the arcane little world that is your local media. Approach your target by inviting them to lunch, coffee, or even breakfast in a neutral setting. Tell him/her what you are up to. You realize he's a media expert and you want to better understand what the local scene is about so that if ever you do have a crisis, you'll know who to turn to. Play to the ego. Remember who you're dealing with. If they are in the media - trust me - they've got **HUGE** egos. Use that knowledge to your best advantage. Most media people will jump at the chance to mentor you, enlighten you, and tell you virtually everything you need to survive and thrive.

Here are some of the things you want to ask (and know):
- His evaluation of other media personalities
- Station/newspaper budgets and finances
- Ratings and circulation issues
- Which outlets are most locally oriented
- Which are friendly to not-for-profits, retail, business, labor, etc.

You want to get an overview of the market on your first visit with your new best friend. If he's been helpful, the next step is to invite him/her to your place of business. If he's not helpful, repeat step one until you find Mr./Ms. Right.

The second meeting, on your turf, is critical. Up until now, you haven't been selling, you've been gathering information. Now you have the opportunity to put your best foot forward. A guided tour of your facility by VIPs, logo cap, key chain, the whole dog and pony show is a good idea. You are now selling your key benefits to him and the community. Why are you so valuable to his and your town? You are hopefully evolving him from skeptic, to acquaintance, to mentor, to ally.

If you do your "schmooze" right, your new best friend is now willing to help you network with other "good guys" in the media (usually NOT his chief competitor). Repeat the process with his referrals and continue networking until you've reached your goals of developing a working knowledge of the media in your town and a working relationship with some of the major media players.

To maintain the desired relations, do follow-up just like you would with any other major client. Think of your media contact in much the same way that you would a major account. You may never make a dime off him but in a crisis his help and knowledge could save your company millions and save your career.

One of the best ways to maintain dialogue with your media buddies is to offer your services as an expert in your chosen field, someone your media pal can call on as a resource.

Here's a great way to become a resource. Let's say you manufacture ice and there's a story about tainted ice cream being manufactured in another town. You e-mail your media buddies an analysis of why it happened there and what safeguards and quality control you employ so that it's highly unlikely it could happen here. This accomplishes a number of things: it keeps you top of mind, gives him a local slant on a story with sizzle; you've done his homework for him so he will appreciate your effort, it reassures the community, and it promotes your brand in a positive manner. AND IT DIDN'T COST YOU ANYTHING! Plus, if you ever do produce tainted ice, you've got a mulligan.

Major players also help you get to the secondary players, the grunt reporters that will probably be first on the scene in a crisis. These folks are either the clock punchers or the ambitious ones. Your media pal can fill you in on which ones to semi-trust and which ones to be VERY careful with. You get to know the beat reporters best in small groups, maybe a catered lunch at your business with a similar dog and pony show that you performed for the major players. They don't have to be your allies - neutral but familiar with your story is good here.

The point of my counterpoint is this: worry less about the media's agenda, which is profit and the story, and more about your agenda, which is to survive and thrive in a crisis.

Chapter 12

DON'T CREATE OBSTACLES

POINT:

It is a legitimate question to ask how you as a spokesperson can create obstacles to good media relations in times of crisis and especially in times of non-crisis. After all, you are likely making your best effort to supply the information requested in times of crisis and hopefully trying to develop good news stories, positive image building, and good relationships when there is no crisis. What more do they want from you?

First, a reporter in a crisis situation will want it all - everything you can give them including unlimited access to your property, your personnel, and all the records you possess (training, financial, safety, etc.). Of course, many of these requests (demands) are unreasonable, often frivolous, and in some cases protected legally from their prying little minds and eyes. But they will ask for it. And they may ask for it repeatedly hoping you'll give in to their persistence. This can almost be guaranteed.

Standing your ground on "unreasonable" requests should not be considered an obstacle in my estimation. The reporter may see it differently but remember they are paid to see it differently. You, as a spokesperson, should not take offense to the complaints of a reporter(s) that are claiming that your reluctance to release certain privileged information is an "obstacle" to the goal of getting "A" story, IF (please note the emphasis) you are providing factual and timely news releases as the crisis unfolds.

Stand firm in your own mind that you are doing a good job in releasing facts and that you have the absolute right to protect proprietary, privileged, or confidential information. Your employer will expect you to do so; otherwise you may find yourself answering to an angry boss, legal counsel, or unemployed.

However, IF (please note emphasis again) you have not provided factual information, a press release or conference, and are not updating information routinely as events unfold, criticism of you and your media policy may be well-founded. This is the first hint of an organization creating obstacles to the reporting of the event and of you making a bad situation worse. Shame on you!

Of course if you stand and deliver "No Comment," you receive an A+ for the course in "Creating Media Obstacles 101." We've already talked about what the message "No Comment" sends and the consequences it creates for you, so why add "obstacle" to that list? You don't have to. You cannot and should not give away the farm of corporate information but you can eliminate obstacle #1 by reviewing and updating your practice and/or policy of "no comment."

Let's assume that you are not the A+ student in Media Obstacles, and you've commented. You are making a good effort to release all the information you can. You are trying to be fair and equitable in assuring that all media outlets have that information. You are trying to provide the video and photo opportunities deemed necessary for our friends working in television, radio, and newspaper land. But you sense something is awry with the mood of the reporters at the scene and you can't quite put your finger on it. Are you creating obstacles?

Not likely if you are, in fact, doing the good things listed above to the best of your ability. Reporters are a moody lot and are never quite satisfied with your best no matter how good it might be. How you view an obstacle is relative to your perspective. Standing at the gate of your plant, school, or building not letting reporters onto your property is a media obstacle. For you, it is your right. (It is, you know.) However, the harshness of your attitude can be softened with some basic thoughts of how you would like to be treated if you were in the reporter's shoes. They are trying to do their jobs just as you are trying to do yours. (Understand that "spokesperson empathy" is a one-sided emotion - yours) However, reporter empathy is an extremely valuable commodity and must be earned. Only then can it be used by you, the spokesperson.

There are some basics in overcoming the obstacles that reporters perceive you are generating. Most of them concern the comforts, accessibility, fairness, and attitude toward them. Many obstacles surface in the longer-term crisis (several hours to several days). Here are **5 Hints to Avoid Creating Media Obstacles** which will promote good will with media representatives. In turn, making you a great spokesperson in their eyes:

- **Hint #1** - Utilize pre-designated staging areas for the media. Have a podium and backdrop that enhances your logo, icon, and brand identity. The TV folks have big, live broadcast trucks that must be parked. They want a place to sit down during press briefings to write and broadcast. They need access to restrooms. They, like police, fire, and medical workers responding to your crisis, may be there a long time. Treating them like the redheaded stepchild is not in your best interest.

- **Hint #2** – Unless your pre-designated media room is made unavailable by the nature of the crisis, you should assure that the room or facility you use for press briefings has good lighting and ample power outlets to allow them to use their equipment. Use this location routinely for updates. Allow equipment to be stored here if desired. (Security is optional.)

- **Hint #3** – Announce your next update time at the end of every briefing. Gather the media in one spot (although this is like herding cats). Give them the same information at the same time. Reinforce your corporate message each time you brief. Be sure to entertain questions. Be sure <u>not</u> to answer "No Comment."
(Ref: CD – "*What Do You Say, When You Can't Say Anything?*" or www.nocommentsucks.com)

- **Hint #4** – Use written press releases as an outline for your comments/updates. Give copies to everyone in the room. Reinforce your company message while assuring that the most current, factual representation of the situation is made. Also provide copies of pertinent documents that support and are favorable to your verbal message.

- **Hint #5** - Although there may be good reasons why you do not want to have video or pictures taken, the media photojournalists working for television or the print media **will** obtain pictures. Help guide them to where the story is and where **you** want them to go. Guide them to safe areas and avoid areas that unduly exploit the crisis or are not germane to the story. If media representatives are allowed on property after the crisis they should be escorted by the spokesperson or designated company representative. You cannot prevent the use of helicopters or long distance photography with high-powered lenses. It is an argument/fight you will not win.

If you are doing the "right" things suggested in this book regarding the preparation of media policy, planning, and relationship building, then being an obstacle or creating obstacles should not become an issue.

Think of the whole concept of creating good media relationships and not creating obstacles in terms that are easily understood by most everyone. Let's use a banking analogy: We all know that we must put money in our checking accounts in order to write good checks later on. It's a bad practice to "bounce" checks. There is a substantial penalty for doing this. You must make a deposit from time to time in order to write the checks you want to cash later.

Similarly, the good will that you create as a spokesperson for your organization in the non-crisis times with various media outlets can create the necessary "balance" in your media account when you need to cash in media checks during times of crisis. In short, if you are making an effort at the front end to promote your organization, you have the advantage of being able to cash in on those relationships when the chips are down and the crisis happens to you.

If you follow this simple logic and take to heart the hints provided above about not creating unnecessary obstacles (especially "No Comment"), you are on the right track to creating an enviable, media savvy organization.

COUNTERPOINT:

Actually, I think you **should** create obstacles. Boy, does that motivate us. It's the incentive the media needs to REALLY go for the jugular.

The biggest obstacle to positive media relations that you can create is an arrogant, dismissive attitude that encourages a highly charged, negative relationship. Your relationship with the press will be somewhat adversarial; it's the nature of the beast. But it doesn't have to reach crisis level if you do your job right. Do it wrong and, well, a little example is appropriate: Remember President Gary Hart? Didn't think so - probably because Senator Hart's presidential bid never got off the ground. Why? Because he turned some nosy, irritating reporting into an adversarial situation, then doomed the relationship by acting like a jerk. His refusal to manage the media effectively in one little instance led to his political demise. The irony is that up until the Donna Rice affair, Hart had pretty good relations with the media.

Now I'm not suggesting that you provide the media with private or proprietary information but, when you're caught with your hand in the cookie jar, saying "No Comment" simply doesn't cut it.

In the case of Gary Hart, when questions of his infidelity arose he could have issued a statement to the effect that all marriages have their ups and downs and his was no exception. He may have used some questionable judgment but he could have stated that he and his wife were in counseling and were working things out and hoped everyone would respect his family's privacy during a difficult time. That probably would have been the end of the story, but Senator Hart didn't perform his "mea culpa." Instead he denied everything and **challenged** the media to find something. We did. Donna Rice, the good ship

"Monkey Business," and Gary Hart became a footnote in history.

Hart created obstacles by not treating the media with respect. You may not like the media and you may think we're a bunch of sneaks and weasels but just like a tornado headed toward you - you will have to deal with us.

The Ancient Greeks called it "hubris" - the thought that you are above the fray and that you are so special, so exalted that even the gods can't touch you. Substitute "the media" for "the gods" and you've got the Gary Hart example.

History is replete with this kind of behavior. Nixon's "third-rate burglary" and Clinton's "I did not have sex with that woman" are other poignant examples of how not to do it. Tell the truth, as you know it. Admit mistakes that could come back to bite you. Above all don't challenge us to find something because we will. No one is above reproach, we all make mistakes. We're human, and so are the folks in the media. The vast majority of people in the media don't have either the time or the inclination to dig if you don't provide them the shovel.

There are numerous ways to satisfy the media's curiosity and need for a story without giving away the farm. It comes down to who is in control of the situation. If you've done your homework as Ron suggests, and have a crisis plan in place that has helped you build good relations with the media, as well as trained and informed spokespersons, designated press areas, timely briefings and updates, written releases and factual data, you won't have to tell us everything.

Unreasonable demands are just that. Most reporters recognize the "bright line" of proper versus improper questioning and respect it. For reporters who do not respect the line, if you've done your media schmooze well, you have plenty of recourse. You can always go over the reporter's head to your new best friend, the news director, and explain that his guy is out of control on this, that you've done everything by the book, there's no more than what appears, and that he's wasting everyone's time. If you try this you'd better have good relations with that news director and be able to back up your claim. And you only want to go over the reporter's head in the most egregious instances. Otherwise you'll come off as a crybaby. Hey, if you get misquoted or don't like the 7-second edit the TV reporter provided - tough! The more adversarial the relationship, the more obstacles you'll face to get your story out.

Something to remember: Since the vast majority of media outlets are owned by major corporations and conglomerates, there is less and less support for the hard core investigative journalist in today's newsrooms. Since the bottom line is the primary motivator, most local news directors today are leery of rocking the boat. If the company I want to investigate is a big client, chances are I'll be assigned another, less volatile story. If you've lain the groundwork for good media relations, chances are you won't have to deal with a reporter's fishing expedition.

During a crisis you can avoid creating obstacles for yourself by following the "**5 Hints to Avoid Creating Media Obstacles**" Ron described earlier in this chapter. But it is your **attitude** toward the media, in crisis and out, that will truly determine your success or failure during a crisis situation.

If you are friendly, forthcoming, genial, and positive in your approach to us, you'll win the day. If you are antagonistic, arrogant, and dismissive, you'll lose. To use Ron's bank account analogy, every time you follow our advice and play the media game effectively you make a nice deposit of goodwill you can cash in when you need it. Play the game your way and the deposits will be few and you'll have little goodwill to draw on in a crisis.

The one thing I hope you take to heart in this chapter is this: It doesn't matter what **you** think of the media for at the end of the day it is **we**, not you, who decide what gets in the paper and on the air. If you work with the media and make cooperation a part of your corporate culture, more times than not you'll survive and live to tell the tale. I'm not saying it works every time but, if you follow our advice, the chances for success skyrocket. Act like "it's my information and you can't have it," "you have no right to it or to be here," or drop the "no comment" bomb on them and you are, simply put, **toast**.

To collect your free gift, worth $75, send an email to: info@mediacrisisgurus.com

Chapter 13

DO YOUR HOMEWORK

POINT:

As a little kid, I hated to be called on in school. Not just because I was a kid, but because I had a slight speech impediment which prevented me from correctly pronouncing the letter "R." I thought this particularly cruel as my first name begins with the letter "R." To avoid the risk of sounding like Elmer Fudd for the rest of my life, I was placed in elementary school remedial speech therapy. This meant I usually had to go to speech class while my classmates were at recess. This early age incentive to earn the opportunity to play rather than be in class encouraged me to be diligent in my "homework" for speech therapy. An early lesson in the value of homework that was applicable much later in my life.

Eventually I got it! After reciting the word "squirrel" very poorly about a million times, I could finally correctly pronounce my name and I was released from speech therapy jail. It was important to my parents and me that I

82

go to recess rather than stay inside doing my Elmer Fudd impersonation. Who would guess some 30 years later that I would be required, as part of my job as Chief of Police, to give countless media interviews, with ample lingering apprehension of my earlier difficulties with the English language? Elmer Fudd went away and because of "homework," I was able to speak in front of groups and hold press conferences and crisis media interviews with some degree of success.

Later on in school my parents continued to bug me about doing my homework. Their continued emphasis on homework seemed to be a real pain in the "you know what" and a waste of precious teenage time. As it turns out, I eventually learned that doing my homework both in school and later on in life would pay dividends. There were many times when I did not do the assignment thinking it was unimportant. More often than not, I was wrong.

You may remember that when you did your homework in school you usually got better grades. You didn't hunker down in the back of the room hoping you wouldn't be called on. Best of all, if called upon, at least you had something to offer and you weren't embarrassed by having to say, "I don't know, I didn't do my homework". (Similar to saying, "No Comment.")

Personally I hated that situation as a kid but it really wasn't life or death. It was just school and my school chums and the teachers were the only ones who knew if I failed that day. There were maybe 30 folks in homeroom at the most. There were no cameras, microphones, news stories, crisis, studios, reporters, press conferences or a viewing or reading audience of thousands knowing that I had not done my homework. Those were different times and certainly different perspectives on the importance of homework.

Right now, I want you to think of me as your mom or dad, bugging you as an adult corporate spokesperson to be sure to do your homework. In fact, right here and now I'm going to help you with your homework just like Mom and Dad may have done when you couldn't figure out the square root of 4,784 (don't ask, because I don't know).

Now listen up here kids! These are pearls of wisdom learned in the school of mistakes that can help you avoid embarrassment because you didn't do your homework before giving a media interview. Here are **Four Lessons Learned** by doing your media homework:

- **Lesson #1 - Educate Yourself**

    If you are reading this book you are likely to enhance your skill level. Congratulations! If you've gotten this far, you have already started your homework and are ready for your lesson. But how you learn can be multi-faceted. Reading certainly works. If you prefer to learn by listening, your learning curve can really be accelerated by utilizing our *"60 Minute Media Manager"* CD which, as the name suggests, can give you some media savvy basics in, you guessed it, almost exactly one hour. (See the special offer at the back of this book.)

There are a lot of seminars offered by those claiming to be media experts. Of course, we make that claim too. What we bring to you in terms of making you better are two things the other "gurus" in the field do not have to offer:

> 1. We believe you will not find anyone that can give you more combined practical experience in being behind and in front of a media microphone.
>
> 2. We offer an interactive training experience within our corporate seminar, *"Managing the Media in Times of Crisis,"* that satisfies the corporate challenge of training groups, individuals, or assisting in creating sound media planning and policy development.

This is the 2-minute commercial for other products we offer to get you started or to help you become a better media spokesperson. If you like the book and walk away with new media skills, you will love the other products as well. All are content rich and emphasize the practical rather than academic world of media relations.

At a minimum, your education should include the skills addressed in this text, how to write a news release, how to stage and present a successful press conference, and a "role play" exercise to crisis interviewing. (www.mediacrisisgurus.com)

- **Lesson #2 – Don't Speak When Unprepared!**
Homework by any other name is preparation. You cannot be effective in either a one-sentence statement or a full-blown press conference unless you **THINK** about what you are going to say beforehand. A lack of preparation is characterized by: "shooting from the lip," "ready, fire, aim," and/or "engaging mouth before engaging brain." When you think you have prepared sufficiently, prepare some more. The extra effort will pay handsome dividends later in terms of how you and your company are perceived.

Being interviewed by the media in a crisis situation is a daunting task for the inexperienced spokesperson. Why make it more difficult by having your mind a blank slate when the lights come up and the cameras and microphones start rolling? The very basics of preparation that cannot be ignored in times of crisis include:

✓ Know what message you want to convey through your statement(s) and say it.

✓ Before you start, develop a script of what you want to cover (in your head or on paper) and try to follow it.

✓ Anticipate the questions that will be asked and, if you have the information, answer truthfully and factually. If you don't have the information, try to find out and provide it at your next briefing.

- **Lesson #3 – Verify Your Facts!**
There is not much you can do to ruin your credibility quicker than to report something as fact and later find that what you said is not true. For example: You are a spokesperson for a company that produces industrial chemicals. One day you come to work and find that the plant is leaking somewhere or, worse yet, you've had an explosion. Your once non-newsworthy plant is now throwing up a toxic chemical cloud into the atmosphere.

Conceivably, this is a really bad day for you as company spokesperson. In an effort to disseminate information quickly, you scurry around at the start of the crisis, hold a news briefing, and report that the cloud is moving to the northeast. You believe this to be true (either by observation or someone telling you this), but you fail to verify it further. In actuality the cloud is moving to the northwest. Oops! You forgot to verify this very important piece of information prior to release. **NOW WHAT?**

Obviously, the consequences of reporting this information without verifying the exact wind direction will cause you monumental problems. **YOUR** major boner here is going to affect the lives of possibly thousands of people to both your northeast and northwest. How much longer would it have taken to verify all the facts to make your story better? Possibly less time than it took to read this paragraph.

The reporter at your news conference may not ask the question if you are sure that your report is correct and will "air" your initial report of wind direction of the toxic chemical cloud as a matter of fact. People hear the report on their televisions and radios and take action accordingly. Those to the northeast may evacuate their homes to avoid the toxic cloud headed their way. Those to the northwest may stay in their homes based on the erroneous, unverified information you have given, only to be surrounded by a toxic chemical cloud they believe is not headed in their direction. So what do you think about doing your homework now? Seems like a good idea to me.

You may think this example is extreme. But don't believe this can't happen because it can and it has. The toxic chemical cloud example is only one of a variety of ways that unverified facts could make a huge impact on those watching your crisis unfold. You have the information that makes this story both factual and meaningful. The reporter is the only conduit to provide your information to the public. You need to strive to get an "A" or "A+" on your homework assignments before speaking.

What does it mean to your employees and their families if you over report, under report, or fail to communicate correct information regarding injuries, fatalities, and where people may be taken for treatment? These mistakes have a huge impact on morale, your credibility, and disaster recovery.

- **Lesson #4 - "No Comment" is a "Cop-Out"**
Perhaps the best example of poor preparation is the spokesperson that relies on "No Comment." **Don't do it!** If you do, you failed in your homework assignment, and you have failed in front of thousands, not just a handful of classmates.

  Actively seek out those who can verify facts within your organization or coordinate that verification with the first responders to your crisis (police, fire, and medical personnel). Find those who have the best first hand knowledge, talk to them directly and be sure the facts are correct before you present them.

  We know what assumptions do. Relying on a third party, "So and so said this and that," won't provide the accuracy you need for a factual media statement. So, before you are interviewed, ask one last time if what you have is correct. Assure that the situation hasn't drastically changed since you drafted your outline for the press conference.

There are other lessons learned and pearls of wisdom throughout the book that will compliment those listed above. If you hadn't noticed, the "No Comment" comment still puts you at the bottom of your class - no passing grade for you for this blunder and lack of preparation.

COUNTERPOINT:

Here's irony for you. I, too, had a slight speech impediment as a kid and had to stay after school to attend speech therapy. My problem was "th's" and "s." While my pals were out playing ball and building tree forts, I was practicing trying not to sound like Daffy Duck. Ron as Elmer Fudd, me as Daffy, we could have made a fortune filling in for Mel Blanc at Warner Brothers.

I think one of the reasons I got into broadcasting had to do with the early speech trouble - perhaps a little over-compensation? Of course, the fact that I've got one of those "Type A" media personalities had, I'm sure, nothing to do with my choice of careers.

Unlike Ron, I loved talking in class, mostly with the other smart-aleck guys in the back row (I always got "C's" in Conduct). Actually, other than French and Math, I participated a bunch in class. Yes, I was a ham even then.

I was not as diligent in my homework assignments as Ron, which is why I tried to hide in French and Math class. I could always fake it in History and English and do well - which is probably another reason why I became a media personality - lots of style, little substance. I found if you've got a good enough rap most people will buy pretty much whatever you say.

It wasn't until after college and my first morning radio show that I began to realize the incredible importance of proper preparation. There was SO much time to fill and listeners expected lots of content. I couldn't fake it for four hours or rely on the music to carry me. I was expected to have lots to talk about each day. Back then there was no Internet with vast amounts of content at your fingertips. The rule of thumb was one hour of prep for each hour on the air. Since I was on for four hours I really had to get into homework, which meant reading 4 or 5 newspapers and a couple of magazines each day. I also had to watch tons of TV so I could talk about that as well. If there was an author scheduled, I'd have to at least skim his book. Musicians meant listening to their latest LP/CD, politicians - their latest rants.

I couldn't use the "dog ate my homework" excuse with all that time to fill so I was forced to prep - and it paid off. People always ask: "Don't you ever run out of neat things to say?" No, not if you're prepared.

That is why Ron and I are so adamant that you prepare for the inevitable crisis and prepare the right way. By "the right way" I mean learning from our experience, mistakes, and advice and executing your crisis media plan when the time comes. Of course, learning the wrong way to manage the media (listening to the "No Comment" crowd) is about the worst thing you can do.

It's like the guy who plays golf and can't break 100. He practices all the time but still hacks it around. More than likely he's had no training or, even worse, training from someone who doesn't understand golf swing mechanics either. He's also probably playing with ill-fitting clubs. No wonder he's a hack. The vast majority of golfers don't get the right advice or the right clubs. To be effective, you need the right tools and the correct advice; otherwise all that ardent practice is at best a waste of time and, more than likely, counterproductive.

So it is with managing the media, which is where we come in. In addition to this book and our "*60 Minute Media Manager*" CD, our seminar "*Managing the Media in Times of Crisis*" gives you the hands-on experience in front of a microphone or camera. We show you how to dress, whether to stand or sit, where to look, and how to talk the talk and walk the walk. We point out how to answer the questions **YOU** want to answer and how to spin, focus, and stay in control. These seminars help you see and hear how you perform on camera in a mock crisis, with both peer and the Media Crisis Gurus' critique of your effort to better help you handle yourself when all hell is breaking loose around you.

The seminars are intensive and enlightening. In most cases those who attend come away with, not only an understanding of the media's agendas, but practical, on camera/microphone experience. You'd be amazed how well novices perform with a couple of hours of proper instruction and coaching.

Using Ron's toxic cloud example - it is crucial to verify your facts - but let's say you've verified that the cloud is moving northeast and you announce it. But while you're advising the media, the winds shift and the clouds move northwest, endangering a different population - now you've got egg on your face. You did your best, you verified the facts, you covered all the bases, and you **STILL** got it wrong. What do you do now?

First thing is to admit the truth - the wind shifted and new plans are being affected. Next, perhaps a quote from someone like Will Rogers to the effect: "If you don't like the weather around here, just wait 5 minutes." Then, more detail on what you are doing **now** to contain the crisis.

Obviously, you can't control the weather - everyone knows that, so admit it - tell them what you are doing to ensure public safety and move on.

The important thing is that you are doing your best to get the truth as you know it out to the public and that you are cooperating with the media. Honesty and cooperation will go a long way to save the day.

Every time you face the media you should prepare a mental checklist:

- Do I know the facts?
- Have they been verified?
- What information is proprietary that I cannot disclose?
- Have I anticipated likely questions?
- Do I have answers prepared?
- What company key benefits and mission objectives do I want to include in my remarks?
- Am I prepared to announce the next crisis update?

If you want to thrive and survive, to live to tell the tale, don't get caught with the "dog ate my homework" response. Just remember how well it worked for you in class. And if you really want to court disaster, just drop the "No Comment" bomb.

Chapter 14

THE DIFFERENCES BETWEEN PRINT, RADIO, AND TELEVISION

POINT:

The easy answer is read, listen, and see. Duh! But we'll continue. . .

Since the beginning of time, man has used a variety of media to communicate with each other. Grunting, cave writings, and the like characterized man's first crude efforts to communicate with each other. Jungle drums, smoke signals, stone tablets, pony express, telegraph, telephone, radio, television, and the Internet followed. No matter what era you examine or what media was used to communicate during any given time period, one thing is clear - people wanted "news." What's happening next door, across the country, and around the world seems to have always been of interest. And what is perhaps even more interesting is that people have always preferred to learn the news in a variety of ways (e.g. speech, visual, written). Thus, the development of satisfying the various senses and the ways we learn brought us to the three primary media formats used today: print, radio, and television.

You could arguably include the Internet as a fourth, but my contention for the sake of this text and our discussion is that the Internet has yet to evolve as a tool of true media reporting. I would concede that you can read, hear, and see the news of the day (instantly) on the Internet, but there are no "Internet" news reporters calling you or showing up at your front door (as of today anyway). What the future may hold no one can predict, but technology will radically change the complexion of news reporting as it has changed it in the past. For today, let's consider the **Big 3**: Newspaper, Radio, and Television.

Let's stop for a moment to consider what we have talked about in previous chapters to better understand the differences in the **Big 3**. If you understand their distinct differences you can use each of them to your advantage, depending on your need as a spokesperson.

The news agendas of each are intrinsically the same - fill a page, fill dead broadcast air, or create a visual story. The methodology each uses to satisfy the agenda is entirely different, because the reporter's needs are different for each venue. Similarly, the way a spokesperson "handles" a reporter from a newspaper, radio, or television should differ. Let's examine the major differences from the view of the spokesperson.

Newspaper

Rule #1 - You will never win an argument with those that have 55-gallon drums of ink and rolls of paper weighing several tons stored in their basement. The old adage of the pen being mightier than the sword is true - except when you are in a knife fight. Despite all the technological advances in electronic media, the written word in the form of newsprint remains the foundation of news reporting in my opinion. Before calling me old fashioned, let me explain why this is my belief:

- Daily newspapers are the staple source of news for most American's who seek story detail and variety.

- Newspaper and magazine news articles, although now transformed after print to electronic format, are usually considered the definitive source of reference material for research.

- People buy newspapers. They are readily accessible, cheap, and give the opportunity to scan for what may be important to any person rather than waiting to see or hear the news in a sequence determined by the programming manager or news director.

- Newspaper reporting seems to satisfy the need of in-depth and ongoing investigative coverage that is not often provided in radio or television.

Let's suppose you buy into the premise that newspapers are the long-term (as opposed to the television or radio quick hit) staple news source for those that can read. Then for you as a spokesperson, the newspaper reporter can become a very important person in your life, both in times of crisis and in times of non-crisis.

For example, if you are a spokesperson for a major corporation, school, college, or government agency you should know that your organization could generate some type of news story (good or bad) most everyday if someone chooses to report it. The good news for you is most reporters don't have time to do this. On a "hot" news day, your good news story won't make the front page and may not make the paper at all. By now you've learned "what bleeds, leads," as the other stories of the day take a back seat to what is perceived as "sexy" for the moment.

You should also know that you do have good news stories available to you routinely. Good things are happening at your company and with employees every day. Perhaps your organization is a great community partner, made great progress in developing a critical medical product, or has made money for the stockholders by the efforts of a great management team. These stories are the good news stories that won't be often heard. But you have your best shot at getting them in the newspaper. Why? Because there is more space, so there will be more days when a crisis will not crowd out your good news story.

When considering how to work with newspapers it is extremely beneficial to develop strong relationships with both the reporters and editorial staff in times of relative calm. This suggestion may sound familiar as Mike covered it pretty well in the last chapter. Believe me, it works.

I liken it to depositing money in your checkbook or savings account knowing that eventually the bill will come due or the rainy day you've saved for has arrived. You trust your bank to safeguard your money. You also believe your money will be made available to you when you need it, and perhaps, you will actually receive some additional interest on your deposits in the future. Eventually, you will withdraw it. If you have a bill and/or emergency and you haven't made a deposit, you are out of luck in trying to escape the inevitable of "paying the piper."

The relationships and trust developed with newspaper reporters may prove to be extremely beneficial to you as they are like you - also putting money in the bank for bills

100

they need to pay or for the "rainy day." Imagine the good will that can be generated by the call(s) you make to the business section reporter, giving him a good news story about your company to fill their column inches on a day when there is nothing else to report. Moreover, think about the positive messages that you as a spokesperson can promote in these types of non-crisis stories. You are, in essence, banking intangible "pay-backs" that you may need to cash in the future when "Mr. Crisis" comes knocking at your door.

In times of crisis, if relationships have been established and the reporter or news outlet knows your reputation, they have favorable history to draw upon and do not have to spend the time and/or resources to learn who you are. They also have some sense of your safety record, personnel training, community partnerships, your overall business track record, and the corporate message beforehand. Using the calm before the storm to perform this spokesperson generated work can pay huge dividends when you are seemingly up to your backside in alligators.

The newspaper also provides you the best venue of the **Big 3** to promote your message in more detail; allowing you to provide more facts that support your corporate message in either non-crisis or crisis situations. Remember too that television generally works off the 7-second sound bite.

Radio may be a bit more liberal with that time frame depending on the formatting of the news programming and the reporter's clout back at the station. The newspaper reporter will likely spend more time with you, as they have more space to fill and the expectation of detail is greater.

Take advantage of this time if offered. It is an ideal time to enhance your position or offer facts to clarify issues which may be the hot buttons of the event itself. It is a more leisurely style of reporting in general, but some reporters will take advantage of the "leisurely" time frame to go on a "fishing trip" or turn a vanilla story into one that sizzles. More time does not mean, "Talk until you can't talk any more." A good spokesperson will know when and how to end an interview. Normally, that point is when you have stated the message and the facts have been presented. Any more than this reveals that the reporter is indeed fishing or you are just rambling.

>Do this and you won't go wrong:
    Good Opening – Message – Good Closing – Stop!

Another positive aspect of newspaper reporting you can take advantage of is offering charts, graphs, or other written material that relates to the questions asked or supports your corporate position. These will likely be included in the final article (or at least some of them).

102

Reporters appreciate being given a visual aid in making their story points - supporting the contention that a picture is worth a thousand words. When providing these types of documents to reporters, be certain they are a sufficient size to be reproduced. E-mailing electronic copies is now the best way to pass on this type of information. Of note, reporters also like this type of information as it takes up column inches, so they may have to write less that day. Use visual aids or provide copies of reports, etc. <u>only</u> if they support your message. The priority is message first, fluff to follow.

You should also understand and know the deadlines reporters must meet for submitting their stories. If you know this and "mess" with the reporter in this regard out of spite or just meanness, I would contend you are creating an obstacle (see previous chapter). Be mindful of deadlines and the needs of the reporter in a non-crisis situation. In the same breath, it must be said that in a crisis situation you should be mindful of deadlines, but be sure you are taking care of business with the crisis first. Hopefully, you have at least given a preliminary statement with updates to follow. Deadlines have a way of extending themselves in times of crisis. **"STOP THE PRESSES!"** can be a very real exclamation.

Deadlines for every publication will vary. If you live in a city with a morning and evening paper there will be two different deadlines in the same day. In these cases, the story may carry over between two to four or more "runs" of the AM/PM editions of the paper. In cities with morning only newspapers, usually the deadline is early evening in non-crisis times. This allows time for the reporter to write the story, have it edited, and submit it for print. In any case, ask the reporter what their deadline is and they will usually tell you.

Conversely, if you know deadlines and know a little something about the paper's circulation you can pick and choose when to release a news item to your advantage (non-crisis only). The best time I've found to make a press release of some controversy which you want to "play-down" is late on Friday afternoon. Why? For all media outlets this is a time of reduced staffing, reduced interest, and reduced readers / viewers. Unless the story has the merit to be carried through the weekend, you may not be bothered with it on Monday at all. However, a story with substance and/or controversy is sure to be picked up on Monday - so be prepared to be contacted for further comment then. The worst thing you can do in times of non-crisis (again for any media venue) is to release a somewhat controversial story on a Monday morning. This will certainly buy you all the media attention you will care to entertain, as all Media outlets are looking to fill the slate the first thing Monday. Because of your actions, you will be at the top of their list.

Radio

I've been interviewed in seven different formats for radio news programming:

1. Taped field interviews.
2. Taped office interviews. (my office)
3. Taped press conference.
4. Live phone interview (usually from my office or cell phone)
5. Taped phone interview (same as #3 except "aired" at a later time.)
6. Studio live interview.
7. Studio taped interview.

Unless you live in a large media market, these formats will likely be the ones you'll be exposed to.

Most local radio stations are either talk/news based or music based. Those that are talk/news based afford the greatest opportunity for you to talk to them in a non-crisis situation and relate a good news story or enhance your corporate message. Music based stations usually have a limited or shared staff of news reporters and will tend to use news wire services, the Internet, or local newspapers for their national news reporting. For local news, once a story and accompanying sound bite (that would be you speaking) are put together, the story and the sound bite are used over and over and over until new stories are developed and the old story has played out. I don't know when that happens - Mike knows this better than I do and will likely comment on it in the COUNTERPOINT section of this chapter. I do know, however, that your sound bite will not usually last longer than 15-20 seconds, a tad bit longer than a TV segment will provide to you. Thus, you have a better chance of expressing yourself but you still need to be succinct because radio reporters will edit as well - looking for the best quote you give them.

In a taped interview (either in the field or office, but not in a press conference), a reporter **may** give you a chance to do a second take if you stumble, get tongue-tied, or just can't get it together for a moment. **May** is the operative word here. The reporter is likely to do this if you have a previous positive relationship of providing them good information, your sound bite is so bad that there is nothing they can use to "air," or they take pity on your soul and give you a "mulligan" out of the goodness of their heart. Don't count on the mulligan. Actually they can use what you said the first time if they are so inclined.

Speak to the reporter, not to the microphone and you will be less nervous. Consider it a conversation. However, it should be a planned conversation, with some thought on your part of what you want to say. Asking before the tape starts rolling what line of questioning the reporter plans to pursue during the taping is a good practice. Equipment failure in radio seems to be commonplace. If that happens and they ask you to do it again, give them the "mulligan," as they will likely reciprocate later. There are tradeoffs in all of this. Remember: Don't let yourself become the obstacle to good media relations.

In a crisis situation the taped radio interview usually happens in a group briefing. The radio folks may ask for more or clarification after the group session. Why? They have more air to fill and their medium of providing news is audio - more talking and more air time to fill for their listeners. If available, I'd try to accommodate these requests but be sure you are just reiterating and detailing your group message or you may be accused of favoritism from other media outlets. You don't want to have to answer to that charge.

Phone and studio interviews differ slightly. My personal favorite was the taped phone interview. In this scenario, I could sit at my desk without distractions. I could close my door and have in front of me any documentation/statistics that I needed to reinforce my message (already planned out in my mind). I also had the opportunity to talk to the reporter or talk show host beforehand (usually the day before) and had some idea of what we were going to talk about. As the session was taped, I could schedule the session at my convenience. Being a morning person, I tried to make these taping sessions as early as possible with the expectation I would be sharp and at the top of my game, while the reporter or host was still waking up. Sometimes this worked and sometimes it didn't. All of this is situational and must personally suit you and the purpose of the interview.

The absolute best thing about doing a taped phone radio interview is that the reporter cannot see your facial expressions, body language, and the occasional hand gesture. They are experts in detecting voice inflection and seem to know without fail when you are less than truthful (the politically correct term for lying). A skilled interviewer will pursue you when they sense (through your voice) they have you on the ropes, or if they are going down a path of questioning that you don't want to go down. This is why it is so important that you prepare for these types of interviews and attempt to return to your message as often as you can - weaving those points into the honest answers you are providing to the questions asked of you.

Taped studio interviews are technically similar to the taped phone interview. This format will require more preparation as you may not have the opportunity to bring supporting documentation with you. If you do, the reporter will likely want to see it and perhaps draw additional questions from it. Thus, you have to know more when entering the studio, unless the documentation you have is something you really want to share. This is usually the case in good news stories. If you have agreed to a studio interview in a post-crisis situation, be extremely careful of what you take with you. A sound knowledge of the facts of the crisis and the ability to convey those facts in an articulate manner are your best friends in this situation. You should also realize the reporter/host has home field advantage. They will be more comfortable than you and can now see all the body language, facial expressions, and gestures that you could conceal in a phone interview. Please don't sweat profusely - it is a dead giveaway that something is up.

If there is a "radio hell" for the spokesperson it is the format of "live" phone or studio interviewing with telephone call-in from listeners. <u>My suggestion is that you don't do it!</u> Especially in a post-crisis situation. Several things could go wrong. You do not want "wrong." Here's what can happen:

First, the reporter/host loves the format because they do not have to prepare and neither of you knows what will happen during the show. (You have no control of questions, irate callers, sabotage callers, etc.) Second, the reporter/host can't guarantee that the line of questioning you agree to / start with will be honored by the callers. You may be stuck with the "Are you still beating your dog?" type of question that literally has no good answer. ("No, I've currently stopped beating my dog but may start again since you've asked this stupid question," or "Yes, of course I'm still beating the dog because of the frustration of being here talking to you.") You obviously lose any advantage you've made in the past regarding your personal and company reputation, but more importantly, you lose any control you might have gained previously. In short, you are at the mercy of the radio audience and the reporter/host.

Television

The thought of appearing on television (especially in times of crisis) can be troubling for the novice or experienced spokesperson. Many would prefer the proverbial "root-canal" rather than appearing on camera. There is this huge camera that is much bigger than any home video device you may have used in the past, and there are bright lights and microphones being shoved in your face or clipped to your clothes. And there is, of course, what you say and the thousands of people that may see and hear you say it. No problem!

Like radio, television relies on the spoken word with an added visual image. This added dimension of video can even freak out some of the most seasoned radio reporters, when reporting news in this unfamiliar venue. Of course, there is the visual aspect of what you look like. My esteemed co-author has what many would describe as the "perfect radio voice" and also a "radio face." Mike has great radio presence, does well in personal appearances and television spots, but will never be considered "anchorman" material. (He could fool me, however.) I've been told that I have a good "TV" face but no one knows quite where my voice is - passable and recognizable in both venues as not quite southern, but not quite Yankee. **(Mike responds: TV reveres the square-faced bland and innocuous, not the exotic Irish good looks that I was blessed with.)** Those being our respective God-given curses or gifts, both of us have had to take our turns at the microphone knowing that what you see and hear is what you get.

This is not a bad thing. Being yourself and professional is really great advice, understanding you have to do this while best representing your company's or organization's interests. You will likely be perceived as genuine, caring, and believable to the viewing or listening audience if you can pull this off. Television extends your message to thousands more people. Learning some of the basic skills in this book prepares you to be unafraid (or at least somewhat unafraid) to stand and deliver before a television reporter.

Television operates in shorter sound bites than radio. **Know this fact.** Local news is normally broadcast in 30-minute time slots. Of those thirty minutes, approximately 8 to 10 minutes are devoted to commercials - which leaves you about 20 to 22 minutes of broadcast time. Then what happens? Of course, they break the remaining time into news, sports, and weather. Then, in some broadcasts, they break the news down even further into national and local news. What do you get for local news in a crisis situation - maybe 5 to 6 minutes or 10 at the outset? Do you think any reporter is going to let you talk a minute or more and expect to have it aired? One minute equates to 10% or more of their total air time for that broadcast. Simply put, it won't happen. So you have to be more succinct and to the point in giving up information. They will edit. They will pick and choose the information you give them, looking for the quotable quote like the radio reporter. You usually get 7 to 14 seconds of air time (I don't know where these multiples of seven come from.) It is not uncommon for a 10 to 15 minute interview to be cut down

112

to one or more 7 second sound bites with the reporter providing the "other" filler.

That is not to say they are not listening and will use other parts of your message as their story, but your television career while on the hot seat will be short lived. Your shelf life as a TV personality will be shorter than you may think. If you do extremely well or do very poorly, people might remember past your 7 seconds of fame. Being remembered for excellence far exceeds that of being known for your unremarkable mediocrity.

How you look does count. You can't be credible in any situation if you look like a clown on air. Business basics will carry you through a television interview. Prior to the interview, have someone look you over who will be frank about how you look. Listen to that person. Leave the cartoon necktie at home or in an office drawer. Don't wear the softball size hoop earrings. A toupee or comb-over flapping in the wind is particularly distracting. Your appearance should never distract from the message you are delivering. If it is, change it. If you are the problem (sorry - no TV face/voice), find someone who can speak for you that you feel comfortable with **and** presents the image you desire.

In this age of instant news coverage and digital recording, the live interview cannot be avoided. The good news here is that you will never be exposed to a live call-in interview on television. They don't work and the TV folks hardly ever use them, as they are a hassle for them to put together.

A cell phone may be the camera and microphone in remote areas that news crews cannot access. Don't worry about what type of camera is used or whether the station is going live via satellite, cable, or whatever. Stay focused on what you want to say, how you are going to say it, and the knowledge you have prepared for the questions that will be asked without resorting to "No Comment."

In closing the POINT on this chapter, two things come to mind:

1. Quotes
2. Questions

There is some commonality of purpose in all three venues when approaching the issue of what quotes the media will use and what questions they will ask. The rule of thumb appears to be: the quote that is most off the wall or controversial will be used first and foremost. Saying, "We are deeply concerned about the large number of fatalities during today's incident." is certainly different than saying, "Well, we seem to be stacking up bodies like cord wood."

114

Which one will be used as your quote? You guessed it.
It's a no brainer.

The "I wonder what questions they will ask?" rule of thumb
is this: They will ask the one question that you thought they
would never ask. **Period.**

COUNTERPOINT:

Ron makes a good point that humans have wanted and
needed the news since prehistoric times. Even then, Grog
being eaten by a cave bear, rather than Oog growing
wheat to feed the tribe was what people talked about
around the camp fire. Humans have always preferred
news of tragedy, pathos, and suffering to "feel good" news,
and so it is today. You may say, "**I'M** not like that and
neither are **MY** friends," but consistently during a crisis,
viewer, listener, and readership ratings go through the roof.
You may not like it, but it is reality.

As Ron said, the differences between print, TV, and radio
are pretty obvious but there are significant differences that
are not so obvious.

> "If it weren't for Philo T. Farnsworth, inventor of television, we'd
> still be eating frozen radio dinners."
>
> - Johnny Carson

The difference in levels of experience of TV, radio, and
print reporters can be huge. As a general rule of thumb,

print and radio reporters have been on the job considerably longer than TV reporters. Inexperienced reporters can be more easily manipulated if you know what you are doing. But, because they don't know the drill, they can also be the most dangerous by reporting irrelevant but possibly damaging info about your crisis. The more experienced reporters usually will stick with the basics.

It is important to note that in many cases experience levels are predicated on market size - the larger the media market, the more experienced the reporters.

For reporters in small to medium markets, this could be their first gig. They are generally anxious to make a name for themselves and it can be at your expense. It's usually easier to get to know the print and radio grunts, as their jobs are less glamorous and less mobile. They are paid less and more grateful for your attention. They can be most helpful to you in a crisis if you've done your media schmooze homework. You really want to get friendly with TV photographers as well (they **do not** like being called cameramen - those are the folks back at the studio.) They can have a lot of influence on what young, inexperienced reporters cover, and they can make you look good or **really bad** depending on how they shoot you. Call them by their first names and they'll be your friends for life. They generally stay in one town, so it behooves you to be nice with them for long-term benefit. Not so with the TV reporters in the small or medium market. They are upwardly mobile, driven to climb the corporate ladder and put another (or their first) notch in their gun. Your crisis could be their ticket to L.A. You really need to handle these folks with care. It has been said that TV reporters are chosen more for good looks than substance but, since I have many TV reporter pals, I won't go there.

"I find television very educating. Every time somebody turns on the set, I go into the other room and read a book."

- Groucho Marx

In large markets, the vast majority of reporters have worked their way up the ladder, the airheads have been weeded out, and you are dealing with quality. Of course, it seems as if every town has a Geraldo - whose head is up when everyone else's is down or vice-versa.

TV and radio anchors and print editors are almost always the best and the brightest of their respective professions. But beware the morning radio talk show host. At least one of these guys in your town will be way out there, the guy who gives the rest of us a black eye - a real knucklehead; creating controversy where it doesn't exist - trying to embarrass you and your company for no good reason other than ratings. You really want to try to avoid these folks. Generally, they won't be reporting on-site at your crisis, they mostly focus on politics and religion. But if they, or their producers, call and want to interview you, find out the ground rules (if you can and there are any) - like whether you will be live, with callers and others asking questions. Assume that the producer is recording your conversation even if he doesn't tell you he is (which, by the way, he is legally obligated to do.) **The microphone is always hot.**

Remember anything you say can and will be used against you in the court of public opinion. The only way to handle this type of reporter is to stick to **your** agenda - what you want the public to know, not what he's trying to squeeze out of you. You will survive the media piranhas if you keep your cool, stay on message, and maintain control.

Another difference between radio, TV, and print is that the electronic media generates most of their leads from the daily paper(s). Why? Because newspapers generally have more reporter resources - more folks on the street, more sources. Use this knowledge to your advantage. Help the print guy to put your best spin on the piece by focusing on your message - say it, say it again, and then repeat it.

Internet "blogging" and "pod casting" are also becoming significant sources for news tips and could be of great benefit or detriment to your message delivery. A good

118

spokesperson will be aware of the influential "bloggers" in his area.

Consider depth of coverage. Newspaper has the most room for your story and TV has the least. In all cases, make what you say count. Print is most likely to revisit your crisis, maybe looking for a new spin or an investigative opportunity. Be prepared for the follow-up - anticipate what comes next. TV has already gone on to the next visual, but you may see "file" footage of your crisis in the future.

Ron wonders why radio tends to play the same embarrassing sound bite over and over. A lot of it has to do with staff size, time constraints, and reporter motivation. But it's mostly predicated on our radio listening habits, especially in the morning drive. The average listener will stay around for about 20 minutes before punching out. Because of that, radio wants to give you the most compelling element it can, hoping you'll hear it at least once. Of course, if it's **your** sound bite, you are much more likely to listen for it and pay attention to it. This philosophy has much to do with why music radio stations play the same 150 songs over and over. Programming is geared to short term listening, playing the allegedly "best" songs ad infinitum with the hope that you'll hear your favorite songs and stay tuned in longer. This philosophy is especially annoying to people who listen for long periods of time and is one of the major reasons for the dramatic increased usage of I-Pods and satellite radio.

Ron also makes a good point about planning for the interview. Don't expect the questions in advance - you won't get them because it is not in our best interest to give them to you. But, if you've done your homework, you'll be able to anticipate virtually anything thrown at you.

I always loved having my interviewees in studio rather than on the phone. It's my home turf. I'm in control. I can look you in the eye, watch your body language, and watch you squirm. I can get more of what I want out of you. Your best defense is to stay on point. Don't be distracted by all the electronics, the bells and whistles, and the man behind the curtain - the media equivalent of the Wizard of Oz.

To collect your free gift, worth $75, send an email to: info@mediacrisisgurus.com

---

Chapter 15

STAY COOL – BE PROFESSIONAL

POINT:

Screaming now seems to be an extremely popular way to present the news, sports, or even the weather. I must have dozed off for a few years and when I woke up, everyone was screaming at each other. Pundit vs. pundit. Reporter vs. interviewee. Reporter vs. reporter. Perhaps this is an extreme cycle in news reporting or, then again, it may just be the true human soul being revealed in formats like CNN, FOX, and (God forbid) the hallowed halls of ABC, CBS, and NBC. ESPN has joined in on the fun and a host of local cable shows and radio "personalities" are screaming their way to fame and fortune as well.

Damn the news. Damn any semblance of professionalism. Damn it all, I just want to scream and belittle my co-host or guest. Now this is entertainment! Thank God for the newspaper. We can take some solace in the thought we're not able to hear the screams contained within those pages (I'm sure they are hidden in there somewhere) as we peruse it over a cup of coffee and a donut on a Sunday morning.

This evolution of the scream-fest newscast gives cause to wonder if journalism schools across the nation have resorted to giving the best grades to those students who can be heard above the screams of their classmates. Although there is some semblance of professionalism left in many reporters in both local and national markets, the screamer is out there. It is a new media career path especially for the cub reporter. They may be employed (ever so briefly usually) in your media market. If they are, **BEWARE!** They will try to suck you, the corporate spokesperson, into their mode of communication - simple, pure, un-adulterated confrontation.

One could make a plausible argument that news is confrontation, or at least an adversarial relationship. I would agree to a point, although it is somewhat contrary to what both Mike and I have stated in past chapters. The media/spokesperson relationship can be cast in two very differing scenarios:

1. The ever righteous media - reporters of the truth - warriors of protecting the 1st Amendment at any cost, in battle with the secretive, deceptive, fact-hiding, less than truthful (e.g. lying) media spokesperson.

OR

2. The always diligent, forever cheerful, give them all you got even on a bad day media spokesperson versus the evil empire of the media - armed with cameras, live microphones, big trucks, obnoxious reporters - determined to destroy our corporations, institutions, and the American way.

Of course neither scenario is entirely accurate. Kick the soapbox out from under yourself if you hold either of these positions dear, and realize that somewhere in between lies the truth about the relationship between reporter and spokesperson.

My experience suggests that media relations are both adversarial and conciliatory. Everyday the reporter and spokesperson play a cat-and-mouse game of information sharing that is not often equitable to either. At this point, it is best to remember that there are two differing agendas - fill the page vs. protect proprietary information. As such, there will always be some controversy and distrust in "news encounters of the worst kind." The "givens" of this situation include:

- Reporters will attempt to get their story.
- In this attempt they will ask questions.
- Some questions will be ones you will not want to answer or believe the question to be beyond stupid, moral, ethical, etc.

- This may make you angry.
- In addition to the questions asked, the reporter's attitude or demeanor may make you angry.
- A screaming or persistent reporter will make you even angrier.
- <u>Some</u> reporters take great delight in pushing your "hot buttons" to see how you will react.
- You know your hot buttons - now, they do too.
- When you get angry during an interview you:
  - A. Say stupid things
  - B. Do stupid things
  - C. Look stupid
  - D. Lose control
  - E. All of the Above

In our continuing quest to educate you about the media, if you answered: **"E. All of the Above,"** you move to the head of the class (for the moment.) This situation is what this chapter is all about. Lost in the discussion of the screaming reporter is the screaming, lame brain, spokesperson who has lost their cool, lost control, and is now a living, real-life, streaming-video example of the person not suited to be a spokesperson. That is, unless your corporate message is one of we seek and employ hot tempered mildly neurotic, loonies at XYZ Company. If you understand this corporate message, please rush your resume to www.youtoocanbeanidiot.com immediately.

Bottom line is this: You must, even under the greatest of provocation, remain professional and represent your company in a manner which depicts you and your organization in the most favorable light possible. Is that easy? No. Can you do it? Yes, with some thought that it must be done. Do the best of spokespersons fail at one time or another? Fail may not be the best word, but most of us falter for a moment or two, despite our experience or how good we may be - we're only human.

Now, let's add the variable of a crisis situation. Stress goes up. Excitement mounts. There may be real (not pundit) screaming. Throw in some fire, flooding, an armed gunman or two, and you've got some real issues surrounding you. We know from experience that in these types of situations the spokesperson cannot remain as neutral as we would like. You may have seen friends and coworkers injured, killed, or missing. Buildings may be burning or destroyed by hurricane, tornado, or earthquake. The trauma you may see in the early stages of a multiple fatality crisis will affect you in ways you do not know until you experience it. All in all, you are likely not having one of your best days. But yet, you have been designated to talk to the media in this time of crisis.

Speaking to the media is probably the last thing you want to do at this time. You do know it is necessary, as it is part of your job and there is a calming, positive message that needs to be delivered in this utter chaos. You should be determined your demeanor will not add to the chaos. You should also know it could. There is little else more disturbing than an emotional company spokesperson. If you can't compose yourself to rise to the difficult occasion of speaking in times of crisis, you should pass the baton to a trained spokesperson who can.

Our contention is if you planned and trained for this moment, it will always be difficult, but manageable. I would also contend, however, if you just can't quite muster the composure you need, ask that you be relieved of your spokesperson duties. Your boss and others should understand the issues of forcing a spokesperson on the air after they have just endured a traumatic event or have witnessed friends or co-workers injured or killed.

If you have been a part of the crisis event and are now ready to change hats from crisis participant to crisis spokesperson (this sounds cold, but is often the reality), the last thing you want to encounter is a reporter who will try to hit "hot buttons" or ask painfully obvious questions which do not merit a response. For example: "How do the families of the persons that have been killed feel?" (This

126

actually was asked of me.) After the initial thought of strangling the idiot, you have choices. As you might have guessed, "No Comment" is not one of these choices. A stupid question does not deserve a stupid answer or angry response. Despite the overwhelming desire to get mad, you have the obligation to try to get past the reporter's ignorance or the issue that is bothering you and spin the question into something that directs you and your audience to your pre-planned message. Granted, you may not always be able to do this.

Sometimes a stupid question or one out of context will be summarily dismissed by the reporter's peers. The consensus is, "How could you ask something that dumb?" Do not count on this happening as, more often than not, the question you consider stupid question will be thought of as a stroke of brilliance by the media peers. You will, without question, know by the other reporter's response whether the informal media jury that has formed has let you off the hook.

In our CD, "*What Do You Say, When You Can't Say Anything,*" we provide many examples of sample statements that support our basic premise of, "you must say something." A statement which buys you time or defers the issue until you cool off is often the best approach in neutralizing a situation that is making your

127

blood boil. Losing your cool is, in two words, not cool. Promise to return soon so that you can fight another day without putting five quarts of stress in your four-quart bucket.

Moreover, the idea that you have remained cool and professional in a crisis only adds to your credibility later. Your peers, your bosses, and the media actually notice these things and will respect your effort. The viewing audience or the folks that read the morning paper will also evaluate your performance. If they give you the thumbs up, then you as an individual have given your company or organization a great image boost. If you get the thumbs down, so will the product or service you offer. Please don't kid yourself into believing that people don't notice – they do. Keeping your cool and showing the world that you are a professional (not a screamer) is the key. If you are at a loss of how to do this in times of crisis use our "*Two Minute Drill*" to get it right:

1. Do you have current facts and have you verified those facts?

2. Are you ready to deliver **your** corporate message?

3. Have you anticipated the questions you will be asked?

4. Do you have applicable handouts?

5. Is the media properly "staged" for your presentation?

6. Do you know which media players will be present?

7. Have you anticipated the "surprises" that go with a press conference?

8. Have you checked for wardrobe malfunctions?

9. Believe you know more than they know.

10. Take a deep breath. Calm yourself. Be confident. Take control.

Want more on this? Check out the "*The Media Crisis Gurus' Emergency Urgency Drill*" CD on the order form in the back of the book.

COUNTERPOINT:

Stay cool and be professional - wise advice and easier said than done - especially if some smart aleck reporter is shoving a microphone in your face while a photographer has his camera so close you can see his zits.

So how do you stay cool in a crisis? One of the reasons pro golfers practice two foot putts for hours isn't because two foot putts are tough to make - they're not - unless you've got to make one to win a million bucks. Talk about stress. Talk about crisis - especially if you miss. The pros spend practice time so in times of enormous tension, muscle memory takes over, which helps negate the stress so they can knock the putt in dead center.

I urge you to follow the lead of top pro golfers and practice, practice, practice. Have your co-workers devise scenarios you might encounter, then hold mock news conferences or interviews with your coworkers acting as reporters. Make sure the exercises are recorded so you can play them back and critique your performance. Just like you have fire and emergency drills, you should practice crisis news conferences at least once a quarter. You can make them fun (everyone likes playing Mike Wallace) but the result should be deadly serious. After all, it is your career and your company's brand you are protecting. Of course, if you need additional professional critique, you can access Ron and me at www.mediacrisisgurus.com for all your coaching and training needs.

Some of the things you should practice:
- Establishing news conference ground rules
- How to take questions from reporters
- Where to look when the camera is on
- How to look when on camera (clothing, posture, voice, etc.)
- Staying on point through distractions
- Focusing on the corporate message
- The use of humor

- Answering the unexpected, out in left field question - the one that is not germane to the issue at hand
- Handling proprietary information
- Warm-up and breathing techniques

The more you practice (I mean **real** practice, not just screwing around) the better you will perform in a crisis. Have your co-workers put you to the test. Make them stretch you so when the real thing happens you can handle the media's slings and arrows. And remember, it is a **performance**. You are center stage. Practice the right way and when the real test comes along you will pass with flying colors.

Staying cool and professional is a lot more than just practice. Just as important is a positive attitude. If you approach the news conference or interview scared, with a chip on your shoulder, with the thought that "it's my information and you can't have it," or "I hate those media jerks, they are making my life miserable," you are **toast**. An angry, defensive spokesperson is the bloody goat in the water to the media piranhas. We just love it when you are out of control, when you hold a grudge, or are just plain pissed off at having to be there. Whatever preconceived notions you might have concerning the media are irrelevant. Forget about it.

It is imperative that you look at any encounter with the media as an opportunity to shine and to show off your corporate colors in a positive way - a way for you to succeed. Like Michael Jordan or Larry Bird who always **DEMANDED** the ball in crunch time, you too can be a prime-time player, but only if you've practiced and your attitude is one of "give me the ball and watch me win one for the home team."

As an example, when playing Little League baseball as a kid, the last thing I wanted was to have the game on the line and me up to bat. I was scared, stressed, and nervous, wishing I was anywhere but where I was. But as I gained experience through playing and practicing, I began to relish being up in a clutch situation. Those experiences helped me to gain an attitude that has helped me innumerable times since in crisis situations, though I still get stressed when I have a two foot putt to win two bucks. Believe in yourself and your ability to stay cool because you've prepared and you will survive and thrive in a crisis.

Now I realize you are a busy executive and you have tons of responsibilities. I've heard you say all the way through this COUNTERPOINT, "Practice - who has time for practice?" Winners, that's who! Take the time, do the prep, anticipate - you'll stay cool and WIN.

Chapter 16

GET OVER IT!

**"You have the right to remain silent.
Anything you say, can, and will be misquoted."
Anonymous**

POINT:

Your fifteen seconds of fame are thrust upon you unexpectedly one day, and you must step forward and act as your company's spokesperson. This could be a very dark day indeed or your moment to shine. On one hand, you may be totally unprepared to do this, by not benefiting from the information in this book or our other info products. In short, you are unprepared - have no company message - yet somehow you just know that your "sharper than a tack" instincts will carry the day. If this is the case, this experience will be a true test for your character and your continued employment.

On the other hand, by heeding our advice you've prepared for this moment beyond anyone's expectations, including your own. You know the tricks of the media trade. You know the media's agenda. You are absolutely sure of your own message and have carefully crafted it so there is no doubt all will read, listen, and hear what you say and be duly impressed by what you say and how you say it.

You call your press conference. The media shows up (much to your amazement). Perfect handouts supporting your message are distributed and readily accepted as fact. You are dressed to impress. The message is solid. You control the question and answer session. You, in your own mind, "nail" the whole deal and walk away thinking what a great media spokesperson you are. Others agree. You did a masterful job. You had them in the palm of your hand. You must show others your secret of handling the scoundrels of the dreaded "press." The evening news looks good and the piece is run again before bedtime. They actually gave you fifteen seconds of exposure. WOW! Life is good. All is well. Until . . .

. . . you pick up the morning paper. You eagerly search through the headlines to find the article about your crisis and how well you handled it. Depending on what happened at your place of business yesterday, that article may make the front page, the front page of the local section, or it may be buried somewhere with the confines of the non-descript black and white columns of news that draws mostly only the comment, "Who cares?" Once you

134

find the headline that describes your jewel of a press conference, you read with great anticipation of how brilliant you were.

You hope they used the handouts because the quotes and information were so good. Much like the late evening news, your skills as a one-time or seasoned media spokesperson sparkle like a diamond amongst the black and white columns that are there only to describe the mundane rest of the world. Your star is still shining - albeit for a few brief seconds.

As you read the article, you find that the news story actually tells your story as you had hoped. They did use the handouts. They name you personally as the company spokesperson and state word for word what you said in a "pre-prepared news release." Looking good Mr./Ms. Spokesperson.

Then the unexplainable happens. You read on, and find the reporter quotes you from the Q & A session. The question is stated correctly but your response doesn't look quite right. You read it again angrily state aloud, "That's not what I said, they've misquoted me. How could they do that to me?" Your bubble is burst. You call friends you know attended the press conference asking if they have read the article to assure yourself you didn't really say what the paper said you said. Those you call agree with you, "No I don't remember you saying <u>that</u>!" Your rage is now confirmed and you contemplate what action you will take. Call the editor? Demand an apology and/or retraction? Sue the newspaper?

Action? Oh, please! Let's look at this a little more objectively than your media star has just been shot from the sky by a star seeking, media owned scud missile. Their weapon of mass destruction - the misquote - has claimed another victim. Objectively, what harm has been done to you or your company as a result of being misquoted?

What was actually misquoted? Was it just human error? (Remember the media Gods are really human.) Did the misquote severely and maliciously damage your message? Or, worse yet, did the misquote make you appear to be uncaring or less than empathetic to the victims of the crisis?

If you are misquoted, get mad - get objective - then get over it. Ask yourself what long-term harm has occurred to you, your company, or others as a result of the misquote. This is truly a judgment call on your part, as only you (or your boss) can judge the damage that has or might occur.

There is a caveat to all this objectivity. If there is a groundswell of negative public reaction to the misquote, this will be immediately evident. If the public outcry is insignificant, then the mis-quote is insignificant as well. This is a good rule-of-thumb: "Significant outcry - significant misquote. Lack of public outcry - insignificant misquote."

Significant misquotes (as judged above) could/can demand action. (Call to the editor, retractions, personal humiliation.) It is a necessary part of damage control. You can take it upon yourself to seek the retraction and attempt to have the correct quote printed in the paper in the next day's issue. Don't count on that happening. If it does, it will likely be buried unless it is a story within a story.

Have you ever read a retraction in a newspaper? One line in most cases. Have you ever heard a retraction on radio or TV? These are less than one sentence, if aired at all. You won't hear, "We are so sorry we misquoted you," "Please accept our apologies.", "We are sorry we shot down your rising media star, great spokesperson that you are.", or "How could we have been so stupid as to make this grievous error?" Bottom line is you won't win the battle with the guys that own the 55 gallons of printing ink and the 300-foot steel broadcast towers. It just won't happen unless you plan to start your own newspaper or TV/Radio station.

I can't remember how many times in my career I've been misquoted. It made me mad. I've called the editor, verbally spanked the reporter, and had to explain to others what I really said. But I hardly ever won those battles. Few do. Why? Because you, as a spokesperson, are trying to win a huge battle from a position of no power. Operating from my position of Chief of Police, the editor, reporter, or news director would listen to me (or at least pretend to pay attention) because of the position I held and the power it commanded. They knew that I could wield some stroke with the other media outlets and perhaps make theirs look bad. You won't have that power base to work from. In short, they may say curtly, "I'm sorry," then hang up the phone and get to the story that is hot today. Your incident is, as they say, "yesterday's news."

I learned that this whole deal of being upset over a mis-quote wasn't a fight worth fighting as the misquote <u>just really didn't matter</u>. Looking at it from 10,000 feet instead of at arm's length and it's not a big deal. Your time is more valuable than to waste it arguing with the media if you just had a significant crisis. Direct your efforts toward recovery and assure if additional issues arise you are consistent with your message. Make the misquote adjustments that are necessary when given the opportunity. How? By bringing the misquote to the attention of reporters doing the follow-up. You can say, "The report of what I said about this in *The Daily Slug* yesterday was inaccurate. What I said is this . . ." Boom! You've made the correction and feel really good until some cub reporter misquotes the correction you just made. Know that these errors will happen. Live with it, unless the misquote is blatant and/or malicious in nature. Then stand up and fight the fight.

There are a hundred stories in the naked city of why you could get mad at the media or a particular reporter. This has been one of them. My advice: unless the misquote is so damning to you, your company, or innocent bystanders/victims of your crisis that it damages individual or company reputations, treat it as a speed bump in the road of life. As my friend, colleague, and co-author would say: "Get over it."

COUNTERPOINT:

I just hate it when I can't argue with Ron on COUNTERPOINT but he really nailed it. Mistakes and misquotes happen — get over it. In the vast majority of cases, it's not malicious; it is incompetence or just a simple mistake. No evil intent, just an oops. It may seem like a huge deal to you but, as Ron suggests, unless there's an enormous reaction to the mistake, live with it and move on.

"Quote me as saying I was misquoted."

- Groucho Marx

Some folks, though, just can't seem to move on. Ron and I gave a presentation to a group of executives in Tulsa, Oklahoma. The participants were into our message. They were attentive and active, especially during the question and answer segments - except for one guy. You could tell from his body language and demeanor that he was angry about something we said.

When I called on him, he nearly bit my head off. He asked how I could defend, let alone be a part of, the degenerate, bottom-feeding, scum-sucking media - the evil empire. Here was a guy who was not happy. In his eyes, everything that was wrong in the world, the USA, and Tulsa, Oklahoma was the media's fault. More specifically, since I was representing the media - it was all **MY FAULT**. The vitriol just spewed from him as he related his story.

Turns out that thirty years ago (that's right, thirty years ago) he was a minister (yes, a minister) of a church in Wichita, Kansas when a horrific event occurred. During the Christmas season, some of his parishioners erected a thirty-foot tall Christmas tree. Tragically, the tree collapsed killing one or two and injuring numerous others. According to our aggrieved preacher, the media had a field day with the event, blowing it way out of proportion by misreporting,

140

misquoting, misinterpreting, and continuing to feature the story long after it had ceased to be newsworthy.

His attitude was that the media should have reported the incident, and then let it drop. He felt that follow-up, like talking to the victims' families, etc., was tasteless and inappropriate. Having only heard his account of the events and not knowing the specifics, I still can state that there are many times that the media beats a story to death. Michael Jackson and O.J. Simpson, etc. - the examples are too numerous to mention. The media senses a juicy story and a feeding frenzy ensues. Unfortunately, it is the nature of the beast and it really sucks when you are the carcass they are feeding on.

That is why it is so important that you know how to handle the media so you can actively work to diffuse the crisis. That is, of course, where Ron and I can be of such value to you. If you follow our suggestions and use our materials, you can succeed in a crisis, it just takes planning and practice.

One of the many ironies of this story is, as our misguided minister related, by utilizing alternative means to get the word out, his church increased both membership and revenue over the long term. The bigger irony was after thirty years, instead of forgiving and forgetting, his vitriolic hatred of the media was still eating him up inside.

At one point in the tirade, Ron jokingly suggested that the preacher and I take it out to the parking lot. Everyone laughed except the preacher. He had never gotten past the event and how the media had allegedly done him wrong. He never got over it and we all felt very sorry for him. Had he not taken it personally, not held a grudge . . . well, it's like being angry at a scorpion for stinging you. It's in his nature - you simply aren't going to change that.

Media people hate misquotes as much as you do. It adversely affects their credibility and without credibility, a news department might as well be "The Daily Show, with Jon Stewart." Fake news. Credibility is the most important element of a news outfit's operation. Lose credibility and ratings and revenues nose-dive.

Take, for example, the 2004 election flap involving CBS News and Dan Rather. President Bush's suspect armed services record (Vietnam era) was being investigated by numerous media outlets. CBS, in a rush to break the story, made factual errors that Rather reported. A firestorm ensued. CBS and Rather were forced to retract the story. Rather resigned as anchor. CBS lost enormous credibility, respect, ratings, and revenue. Rather, as managing editor, took responsibility and blame, but the fault lay with the reporters, editors, and producers who didn't thoroughly research their sources. Dan basically just read the report on the teleprompter.

In most news organizations, a story is vetted (analyzed for credibility) at least four times before it makes it to air. The anchor has very little to do with the actual formulation of the story. The vetting process is a crucial element in maintaining credibility. It enables a news department to get an accurate story, to C.Y.A., but with numerous people involved in the process it leaves more potential for human error. In the case of CBS, the feeding frenzy concerning the story and overzealousness in trying to be first, led to errors in judgment and ruined careers.

Calling into question a news outfit's credibility can be effective, but only if it's a huge deal and you have all the facts on your side. Otherwise, act professional, let the reporter know privately he made a mistake, and more likely than not, he'll feel responsible and treat you a lot better the next time. Above all, don't let the grudge fester for thirty years - get over it!

Chapter 17

CRAFTING YOUR MEDIA MESSAGE

POINT:

It is sometimes not easy to make lemonade from lemons. Finding yourself in the middle of a business crisis which involves an explosion, fire, tornado, hurricane, and even injury or death is not a situation that allows us to look at the silver lining of the cloud which has darkened the day, and possibly leveled our plant in the process.

If you are embroiled in a discussion of company corruption and facing angry investors, stockholders, and past/potential customers, it is hard to muster the words which will allow you to continue down the path of profitability.

In short, when faced with disaster, many of us will succumb to the overwhelming emotion of what is going on around us. We often cannot detach ourselves from the disaster to even think about what we might say about the events that have caused our own little world to fall apart right before our eyes.

Unfortunately, those outside our world of disaster are extremely curious about how our world "came apart," what caused it to happen, and how we are trying to fix it. Moreover, that curiosity is readily recognized by the media as a story (possibly the story) that needs their attention. You soon realize (much to your dismay) the reporters are on their way to probe, poke, and pry into your crisis, which will, in turn, support their pontification as being the conduit of the truth because they say it is so. Please do not kiss the ring at this point - it is undeserved.

What this really means is that the media cavalry is headed in your direction to seek their story (as you know) and will expect you, as the company spokesperson, to say something about what's going on. These inquiries will happen no matter how badly you feel, how emotional you are, or if your crisis is still "hot" and has not stabilized. Your media policy (yes, you should have one) should designate a person or persons to act as spokesperson. Part of your recovery plan should include media relations, so "No Comment" won't work unless you just want to buy ill will. If you have done some homework (Chapter 13) and some pre-planning, this task (making a statement in times of crisis) may not be as daunting as it first appears.

The role of media spokesperson is a role of leadership. You may not have the title or salary which would indicate you are leading, but you just need to look behind you to see that all those employees counting on you to do something. You must promote recovery and ensure their future job security and welfare of their families. This is leadership, plain and simple. You take the "point" position and for those moments "on air" you absolutely take on the role of leader. There is responsibility attached to this leadership. You have been passed the leadership baton by either design or default.

Needless to say, what you do with the baton is important. An unprepared leader is no good to anyone. Neither is an unprepared spokesperson. Giving the interview or press conference without knowing of what you are going to say and how you will say it is like strapping a nuclear warhead to an unguided missile. Something really bad will eventually happen, but you don't know where, and you don't know when. The unguided word has this type of impact - no good will come of it.

The "message" is far more important than the messenger in a crisis. Looking a little battle worn on camera from being a "player" in a crisis situation and not having the red tie, blue shirt, freshly pressed trousers, and shined shoes may not be all bad. But if the message fails to tell the story you want to tell, the whole deal flops. If your responsibility to take the leadership role as spokesperson has not been internalized, **and** if you do not prepare a message that promotes the silver lining this very dark cloud hanging over your business, you will be hung out to dry by the media covering your story.

The "how-to's" of crafting a media message that provides both facts and a compelling corporate story may prove a test of your creative thinking/writing and verbal skills. There are some basic guidelines you can use effectively in most any situation which could carry the day for you. Trying to making lemonade from lemons will include:

1. **Go to the Balcony**

    I like this term better than looking at things from 30,000 feet. It's a phrase that Ron Heifetz uses in his book "*Leadership Without Easy Answers.*" In leadership terminology the balcony is the place to look down on the dance floor of management issues we are routinely embroiled in. Going to the balcony from time to time gives a person a fresh look at the turmoil below. It provides a breather and a different perspective. When finished with the balcony visit you can then throw yourself back into the dance we call life a little more refreshed.

Similarly, the spokesperson, before speaking, should remove themselves from the dance floor (the crisis) to the balcony, take stock of what is happening on the entirety of the dance floor, breath deeply, regain composure, and steal an additional moment to plan their next action step(s) (i.e.; message preparation.)

The balcony should be closer than a 30,000 feet view, but not too close to the action taking place at hand. I'm not saying mentally "check out". ("The spokesperson has left the building.") You being detached (but involved) creates a better defined nexus to the crisis itself for those observing you. This will be interpreted by reporters as you knowing the intimate details of the crisis and also that you do, in fact, speak for your company. These factors enhance your credibility and the validity of your message. Use the balcony as a point to revitalize yourself, plan, and prepare for the important responsibilities you are about to take on when the lights come up, the cameras roll, and the microphones are shoved in your face.

2. **Show Empathy.**

"The bodies are stacking up like cord wood" is not an appropriate empathetic message. (an actual quote by a police commander) The empathy for victims and sympathy for their families should be genuine and be an integral component of the corporate message. Convey this in a manner that convinces others that you feel the same way as the affected individual. Sincerity is the key. Anything less than a sincere expression of these thoughts will be discounted by the media and the public as merely a perfunctory attempt to gain public approval.

In this message crafting, include what your company is doing for the victim's families, how they are cared for, relief funds being established, and other good things that are happening in the aftermath of the tragedy.

3. **Know Mission, Value, & Vision Statements**

    This is what we would consider a no-brainer. What do you do as a corporation? What values do you hold dear? How important are your employees? Where do you want to be today, tomorrow, and in the future? Don't know these? Learn them. Learn them well. Use them as a fall back position of strength when you get "stuck" with a tough question or don't know where to start in crafting your media message.

You must state the facts of the crisis as you know them, but you also must pass on what is happening to support the mission, values, and vision of your company. You could liken these to the guiding light or due north on your corporate compass. These statements are the underpinnings of your media message. As you do your homework and if you see that you might not have these in place, make sure they get drafted first. Having them committed to writing will make your job as spokesperson far easier. They make great handouts as well.

4. **Display a Positive Attitude.**

About what? About everything.

- How things are going now (find the positive in the worst of situations)
- How you will recover and serve customers
- How you will fully investigate ASAP
- How you will assist and aid the victims
- How you are planning to rebuild
- How you are cooperating with first responders
- How glad you are to see the media (**NOT!**)

A positive attitude in message preparation gives hope in times of darkness. You may be crushed inside, but the message of hope and confidence can go a long way in cementing good relationships for company branding and market share in the future.

5. **Buy Yourself Time When Necessary**

    If you were to plot a crisis situation on a timeline continuum, media messaging at the left side (beginning) of that continuum will look slightly different than what it will look like as time moves to the right. The basic value, vision, and mission message will not change, but you as spokesperson may have to buy yourself some time to rethink certain specifics of the message for a variety of reasons.

    Why? Because often, in the early stages of a crisis, you don't have all the facts you need to state the "full" message, as you would like it to be stated at the end. This can be done in a variety of ways and is perhaps better outlined in our CD, *"What Do You Say When You Can't Say Anything?"* This messaging technique is primarily about letting people know that you really don't know everything at this time and you don't want to speculate, guess, or provide information that may prove to be false later. Sounds like you are doing the old soft-shoe.

Perhaps you are, but your apparent shuffling will pay dividends later when more factual details can be disclosed with greater certainty.

Please do not go into any press conference or interview without thinking about what point (message) you want to communicate. You should always attempt to get back to the basics of **your** (not the reporter's) thoughts. It is all about who is controlling the interview. The best interviews I've seen allow the reporter to probe, pry, and poke, then the spokesperson gives an answer, but always manages to tie their answer to the overall message they have planned to promote at the outset. You and the reporter both walk away feeling the goal of the interview has been accomplished. A classic win-win situation. And you didn't have to say, "No Comment!"

Counterpoint:

Ron is right about the spokesperson is a leader. Whether you have the title or not, for that moment in time you are the organization. You represent the brand, the history, the people, the mission, and the vision of the organization, whether you like it or not. Are you prepared for it? Are you up to the task? It is imperative that the mission, the history, and the direction of the organization be indelibly imprinted in your brain so when the crisis hits, you are absolutely prepared to succeed.

If you are a company spokesperson I highly advise you to start every day thinking: "Is today the day the crisis hits, and, am I ready to effectively deal with the media?" Then, in the shower or driving to work, do a quick mental checklist of your company's key benefits to the community, a mission, history, and vision review, and whether you are prepared to us - because today could be the day.

If today is the day, are you ready to lead? Everyone in your organization from the CEO to the janitor will be looking to you for leadership. Your response in a crisis will set the tone for the organization. Leadership means centering your emotions on the "now," exerting control and guidance, and being the calm center in the eye of the storm. You lead by example. If you panic, show fear, anger, or petulance, then you lead your organization down the tubes and the crisis magnifies. If you've got your act together, it's amazing how everyone else follows suit.

A good example of effective leadership in a crisis was Frank Keating, Governor of Oklahoma during the 1995 Murrah Building bombing. Granted, he was Governor and as a politician he was trained to handle the media. But the way he led stands in stark contrast to how most politicians handle a crisis (President Bush's first few hours after 9-11, for example.)

I'd gotten to know Frank a bit when he was an Oklahoma State Senator and had interviewed him on numerous occasions. He's a gregarious, upbeat person - basically a good guy no matter what you might think of his politics. Keating is also the kind of politician who shoots from the hip, or the lip, and some of his off-the-cuff (smart-ass, if you will) comments as Governor had caused a stir on occasion. So, here's a personality who knows the media drill, is highly trained, but his sense of humor and lack of political correctness make him a bit of a loose cannon.

Governor Keating handled the Murrah Building bombing as well as I've ever seen anyone handle a crisis. Inside, his emotions must have been off the chart, but his public persona was a caring, compassionate, yet strong leader. Frank's an old FBI guy, so he must have wanted to grab a gun and take out the scum that did the bombing. But he kept his emotions in check and helped Oklahoma City, the state, and the nation stay calm. He was a wonderful representative for a state that doesn't always show its best to the rest of the nation. During that crisis, Frank Keating made Oklahoma proud.

Now I know you are saying, "Yeah, but this guy was FBI and a professional politician - he's bound to represent himself well." Oh? Then what about Nixon's "I am not a crook," Bush 41's petulant live interview with Dan Rather, Clinton's Monica routine, or Bush 43's famous seven minutes after he was told of 9-11?

Keating's demeanor, control, and leadership are a template on how to handle yourself and the media in a crisis. Keating did hundreds of news conferences and individual interviews during the weeks of the crisis, answering the same reporter questions over and over and not only maintained but thrived. You didn't see the smart aleck or the partisan politician, you saw a man speaking and leading from the heart with compassion and strength - the attributes of a true leader.

Keating had been preparing his whole life for the Murrah Building bombing - you don't have that luxury. But you can still be well prepared for your crisis. As Ron suggests, go to the balcony to gain perspective and emotional control. The media can wait a few minutes as long as you make sure you get with them at a specified time (make sure they know when.) Be human, show controlled empathy, know the crisis drill inside and out, and above all maintain a positive demeanor.

By the way, you can always buy a little time by announcing what time you will make a statement. Make sure the time frame is reasonable. Don't use this as an excuse to not meet with the media or we will find others to interview, usually your competition or a disgruntled employee. Ten or fifteen minutes works well, no longer than thirty. Besides, if you've crafted your agenda well, you'll look forward to meeting the media because you'll be ready for anything.

Chapter 18

TELL THE TRUTH

"_Honesty_ may be the best policy, but it's important to remember that apparently, by elimination, _dishonesty_ is the second-best policy."
                                        - George Carlin

POINT:

Let's do some soul searching here and a little physical exercise to start this chapter. Here goes:

Instruction #1 - Anyone who is reading this book who has ever told a lie in their life must, at this time, stretch open all their fingers on both hands and put their hands straight up in the air over their heads very quickly.

Instruction #2 - Now pick up the book you dropped and we will continue.

As Church Lady might say, "Well now, isn't that special!" What fun we are having now. The former cop is still playing, "Drop the book and put your hands in the air where I can see them." Sorry, that's not what we're doing here. I know this: If you followed the above instructions to the letter and didn't drop this book you are lying.

This roughly translates to: "If you tell yourself you have never lied in your life then you are lying to yourself as you read this text." The point is we all have lied in our lives. No one is immune. Step up and admit it and we'll go on with the discussion of telling the truth to the media. Okay - feel better now?

No one likes the dreaded "L" word, especially when it is associated with them in some way or with what they say. Do you like "less-than-truthful" better? I don't, but it seems to be more politically correct than calling someone an out-and-out liar. There are a host of names for liars. Look it up in a thesaurus. You can water down the name of those who deliberately (key word) do not tell the truth in a dozen different ways. I will leave the popular juvenile taunt of "fibber" out of the discussion for now.

Which brings us to the possibility of someone in the reading audience pointing out to me that there are various "degrees" of lying (sorry, being less than truthful.) Is this true? Perhaps we should have a color-coded liar alert similar to the terrorist alerts that the Department of Homeland Security uses. I can hear the discussion now, "You know (insert name here) is usually 'green', but today when he gave that media interview, his alert went all the way to 'orange'. Man, for a minute there I thought we were going to 'red'. I tell you, if his lips were moving he was lying."

Is a "little white lie" different than committing perjury after you've sworn to tell the truth, the whole truth, and nothing but the truth? Some would argue yes, but let's get beyond that philosophical question and agree on a single point when speaking to the media: <u>If you knowingly provide false information to the media with the intention of covering up something or purposefully misleading them, you will, without a doubt, become the meal of choice as the sharks circle for the kill.</u> If you don't believe this, look no further than the less-than-truthful statements made by former Presidents Richard Nixon and Bill Clinton. If the President of the United States can't get away with it, do you think you can?

Now that I've kicked my soapbox out from under me about the "L" word and its ramifications (it's a cop thing), I'll bring you back to the real world of you being a media spokesperson.

Mike will likely argue this point but, in the world of news reporting, there is a difference (for both spokesperson and reporter) between <u>telling the truth</u> and <u>telling all you know</u>.

You <u>do not have to tell all you know</u>, but when offering up factual information that supports your message or answering questions, <u>you need to tell the truth</u>!

Countless times reporters came into my office to interview me when I already knew who they had interviewed, what was asked, what the responses were, and much of what they already knew. Depending on what was at stake and my time constraints, I would take the opportunity to test the veracity of a reporter's truthfulness. I would pose questions to them (a role reversal) to see if they would be forthcoming with the truth, as I believed it to be. It was a simple pass/fail verbal polygraph. It was also a trust litmus test with whom I wanted to share information in the future.

And guess what? They did the same thing with me. They would throw a question out that they already knew the answer to in order to see if I would be truthful. Eventually you will sense when this is happening, just as reporters can sense it happening to them (at least the smarter ones can.) This "game" of verbal judo can be damaging or deadly to your message delivery and should be taken very seriously, as you know that the "microphone is always hot" and "off the record" hardly ever is. If you slip up here, you will not be misquoted; you will be crucified if the reporter so chooses.

The caveat to this cat-and-mouse exchange is in asking the best/right question(s). As you must tell the truth, but not necessarily share all you know, the challenge is to ask the right questions, and know which of those questions to pursue until you are satisfied you've gotten the whole truth. If I failed to ask the right question of a reporter - shame on me. If a reporter failed to pursue a revealing line of questioning I didn't want to discuss, I walked away relieved, knowing my message delivery was good enough to close most of the doors where skeletons may have been hiding.

This is not lying. This is not selective truthfulness. This assumes you will control the interview, prepare the message, and are being truthful in responding to the questions that are posed. If there are probing questions that could be asked and are not, don't take on the responsibility of shouldering the reporter's job of exploring all possible avenues of a story. This is how news reporting works.

I have never heard of or seen a person being interviewed suggest to a reporter questions the reporter didn't know to ask, should have asked, or failed to ask.

"Oh, excuse me Ms. Reporter, you forgot to ask if I was still beating my dog? I do want to answer that if you will please give me the opportunity."

I have seen, however, many interviewees offer clarification questions (for the reporter), other information, or facts as outlined in their press release or interview that clearly supported and restated their corporate message. This is all well and good. If you know to do this or even think about doing this you are coming of age as a spokesperson.

There are, at times, statements of fact that are released by a spokesperson as being true and accurate which are later found to be inaccurate. These "misstatements of fact" would be considered by some as lying. If you don't attempt to correct these statements there is some validity to that claim. But before you jump to any conclusion about whether the spokesperson "lied", first consider these factors:

- The spokesperson may have been given bad information and believed it to be true at the time of release. (For example: Were there 32 or 35 injured?)
- Continuing investigation indicates the initial belief of cause or outcome of a situation is discovered to have been incorrect. (Example: Human error rather

than the previously reported equipment malfunction was the cause of the accident.)

- Just as reporters misquote, spokespersons make mistakes. We, despite our best efforts, remain human.

In any event, the misstatement of fact demands that the spokesperson attempt to correct their error or they be deemed unreliable or a liar. Just as misquotes have varying impact on the perception of how a story plays out, so do misstatements of fact. Learn to know what will have the most impact and strive to get those errors corrected quickly so the overall corporate message is not damaged in the translation of the information a second time around (if given the opportunity to correct.)

So let's review. We all dropped our book early on in this chapter. We then picked it up and went on to learn that while you are crafting your media messages you must be truthful and factual.

- However, all that you know about any given situation does not have to be provided to the media.
- But, if a sharp reporter asks the right question(s), you should be truthful, answer the question to the best of your ability (without adding fuel to the fire), presenting the facts, as you know them.

- <u>And</u>, you never want to lead a reporter down a story line path unless that story line supports your corporate message.
- <u>Of course</u>, there will be times when you will make misstatements of fact as a spokesperson. Regardless of who or what caused you to make that error, stand up, raise your hand (again), and tell the nice reporters you made a mistake and you would like to tell how that occurred and correct it.

"Truth is mighty and will prevail.
There is nothing wrong with this, except it ain't so."
–   Mark Twain

COUNTERPOINT:

We learn in childhood if you do something wrong, blame it on your little brother. Lying and getting away with it is infinitely better than telling the truth and getting punished. Pain avoidance is a great motivator. So we try to shift the blame, prevaricate, obfuscate, and fib to avoid consequences, right? Or as Churchill described it: "Terminological inexactitude."

So how well did that work for you? If you were like me, you weren't a good liar, you got caught a bunch, and you got spanked, grounded, etc. until you finally caught on lying didn't work so well.

And so it is as a spokesperson. Lie to the media and eventually you will get caught and spanked. Make a mistake and admit it - not much of a story, no legs. Lie and cover it up - Letterman and Leno are **STILL** doing Nixon jokes, to say nothing of Clinton/Monica bits. Cover-ups never go away. Want to be answering media questions two years after the event? Lie about it!

Ron makes a good point that you don't have to tell the media all you know. Be selective. You can craft an answer to virtually any query that enhances your organizational mission and supplies enough factual data to mollify us pesky reporters without giving away the farm. In fact, the technique of irrelevant information overload (cops, generals, and politicians are adept at this technique) where you use statistics to obscure the real issue can be a very effective way to answer a question without answering it.

"There are three kinds of lies: lies, damn lies, and statistics"
- Mark Twain

I don't recommend the irrelevant information overload technique unless you are a well-trained seasoned spokesperson. You may slip and give away proprietary information and really have a problem.

You don't have to answer everything we throw at you. Naturally, reporters want it all, but we'll almost always settle for a good story. Effectively answering the question without answering the question is a true art form. One of the best at this is Condoleezza Rice. Watch her on one of the Sunday morning interview shows. She's on point, forceful, gracious, interesting, compelling, and passionate. She represents her administration well, but never answers a question she doesn't want to answer.

Watch her in action. You'll see while the media guys may get a bit frustrated if she doesn't answer the question they've asked, you can tell how much they respect her and her ability to handle them. She knows her agenda, she reiterates key points, and she does not allow the interviewer to control her. She does a marvelous job of neatly avoiding the pointblank question, sometimes with irrelevant information overload, most often by answering the question she wants to answer not the one the reporter posed. Deftly evading hard questions helps you avoid getting caught up in a lie.

I do want to touch on what Ron referred to as the cat-and-mouse exchange, where you try to determine the reporter's honesty or the reporter attempts to test your veracity. This is a perilous arena for the uninitiated. You'd better have a ton of experience before entering into the type of exchange Ron describes and you'd better know that reporter's track record well. There can be major consequences if you come across as trying to one-up the reporter. He won't be

166

a happy camper, he will make sure his media brethren know you're acting like a jerk, and your well-crafted media relations campaign will be toast. As a Chief of Police, Ron had standing, experience, credibility, and clout. You probably don't. So play the honesty card and you'll win the hand.

To collect your free gift, worth $75, send an email to: info@mediacrisisgurus.com

Chapter 19

<u>SURVIVING, THRIVING AND DYING</u>

POINT:

It really doesn't matter in the whole scheme of things how you might perceive or feel about the media. They are an integral part of life as we know it. If there is a crisis, media representatives will find out about those events and will likely respond to get the story. We propose this set of facts to you as a "given." How well you deal with that eventuality is what this book is about. If you've bought, borrowed, or stolen this book you must have some interest/disdain /distrust/appreciation/knowledge of what the media is and does. Minimally, we hope that you get a basic skill set of knowledge and interpersonal tools which will allow you to survive media inquiries, interviews, and press conferences.

Recognizing that thriving is far different than surviving, we want to give you a few additional "pearls of wisdom" that you can use on a daily basis or in times of crisis because that is really the level we would like you to be (thriving). This book, our other training materials, and the on-site training seminars, *"Managing the Media in Times of Crisis,"* gives us the opportunity to provide a host of information which will allow you to go beyond "surviving" and into the realm of "thriving" when being interviewed by a reporter or having the opportunity to present your corporate message in a press conference.

The survival stories of those we coach are satisfying. As a result of seminar role-playing, we routinely see those with no media skills at the beginning of a seminar session begin to quickly assimilate the information provided, and by the end of the seminar they can "survive" a taped media interview. (Conducted by the ruthless Media Crisis Gurus themselves.) There is no slack given in this role-playing and folks do survive, sometimes even thrive with very little training.

The accounts of clients who have thrived make all our efforts worthwhile. We work with clients in both the private sector and government. As you might guess, we target those who we believe have the greatest probability to be thrown into a crisis media situation. One of the industries we have worked in is the petro-chemical industry. Since the terrorist attacks on 9-11, the petro-chemical folks have received more than their share of scrutiny from Uncle Sam and the media in general. They operate plants that are considered by some as ticking time bombs. Thus, they are keenly aware that what happens at their plants will draw instant media attention. If prepared, this attention can help you "thrive" rather than just "survive."

Mike and I recently presented our seminar at a mid-western ammonia/liquid nitrogen production facility. Not a huge place by petro-chemical standards, but one that just by the nature of what they do, is of sufficient size to draw attention if there were to be an incident. The plant has a great safety record and was virtually "incident free" in the last ten years. They brought us in to train some of their first line/middle managers after some of their upper management had attended another one of our training courses.

There were about 10-12 individuals in our session. All but a couple had no media exposure or no media training. There was a huge distrust of what the media was all about. Fortunately for us, they liked Mike and did not harbor the resentment for him and his profession that we found in other places (see Chapter 16). The training went well. Those that distrusted the media beforehand may still have distrusted the media at the end, but they did gain demonstrable skills that we saw in the final role-play that allowed them, in our opinion, to "survive."

Several months passed and sure enough this plant had a small ammonia leak. It was not large enough to cause great concern to the community surrounding them, but was large enough to get HazMat teams rolling to the site which, in-turn, brought media trucks and reporters out of the woodwork. Watching the news that evening we recognized one of our class participants doing the interview. To say he "survived" would be an understatement. He got the normal 7-15 seconds, but even during that short period of time he created the very sound corporate message that "all is well." His message centered on: "There is no need to worry now or in the future. The leak today was no more than a speed bump in the normal production of our product. Thank you very much - please leave us alone so we can continue to contribute to this community as good corporate neighbors." Wow!

The in-depth coverage in the newspaper the following morning was even better. We sent the spokesperson a short email expressing what a great job he had done with the interview. He wrote back relating that he had indeed thought about many of the ideas we had given him in the training and how he had used those in message preparation and in conducting the interviews with both the television and newspaper reporters. Talk about "thriving." Needless to say, we were extremely pleased knowing that the seminar had paid instant dividends for him and his company.

If you want some more "quick-hitters", here are the "*Media Rules to Live (and thrive) By,*":

- Tell the truth, as you know it.
- Release only confirmed facts.
- Be concise.
- Show genuine concern for the situation, loss, and victims.
- Defuse rumors - tell the story you want told.
- Remain calm - don't add to the chaos by your demeanor.
- <u>ACCEPT RESPONSIBILITY WHEN IT IS YOURS</u>.

Your preparation in a crisis media situation should always be preventative in nature. You don't know if you will ever be called upon, but you want to be prepared if you are. You have to ask yourself the question, "Do I want to be caught up in this situation and be unprepared?" Well, do you?

This brings us to the subject of "dying." Fortunately, we have no war stories of our students dying on the vine in the middle of a media interview. That's not to say it couldn't happen. Simple things like engaging one's mouth before one's brain can make you road kill in a heartbeat. The deer in the headlight look as you freeze up when the camera lights come up sometimes can't be overcome. But we do know that there are certain things that will kill the interview and your chances of success if you do them. We call them, *"Media Rules To Die By"*:

1.   Show a lack of empathy
2.   Speculate, Over/Understate, Showboat
3.   Inadequately Prepare
4.   Respond to Hostility with Hostility
5.   Blame Others for Your Mistakes
6.   Reveal Confidential or Proprietary Information
7.   Give "Exclusive" Interviews or Show Favoritism
8.   Talk Off the Record

Do these things and your world during or after a media interview will not likely be a pleasant place to reside. Fair warning has been given. We won't say "We told you so," but. . . "We've told you so." Oh - almost forgot - there is one more "Media Rule to Die By" you might already recognize - please read on.

Counterpoint:

It is extremely gratifying to see one of our clients use the tools and advice we provided to great success, as Ron presented in the preceding example. That client took our advice to heart, and an enhanced standing in the community was the result. No panic, no fear, no confusion, just an honest, straightforward response to a crisis - a response that had a positive impact on the company brand.

Our media rules to live and die by are battle tested. They will work for you if you use them properly. That means understanding them conceptually, practicing them, internalizing them, and practicing them again.

Our rules to live and die by are pretty easy to summarize and remember: be calm, concerned, truthful, prepared, to the point, accept responsibility for your actions and don't let your ego get in the way of your message and your mission. Yes, they are common sense; no it isn't brain surgery. But it is amazing how many people lose their careers because they didn't heed these simple rules to live and die by.

We will get to the super-sized rule to die by in the next chapter, but another rule you need to heed is avoiding a trap we media people love to set. That is the hypothetical, speculative question, the good old "what if." I'm constantly amazed at the number of times reporters can make this work. A lot of times the spokesperson isn't prepared for the hypothetical because as it is usually asked out of context. For example: "What if the fire had reached the nitroglycerin tank, could it have taken out the west side?" You don't have to answer this question. You handle it simply. "It is not my job to speculate on your hypothetical. You might as well be asking what I'd do if an asteroid fell on the plant today. Next question."

You do not have to tolerate questions that ask you to speculate. We reporter folk love to con spokespeople into speculation. It opens up all sorts of avenues to probe. It makes for great quotes for me, but not necessarily for you. Don't fall for the trap. You can't win. Be calm, be nice, but be emphatic: "Sorry, I will not speculate - that's your job as a pundit - that's what you get paid for - and I certainly wouldn't want to take away your livelihood. Next question."

We media types are also a sneaky lot, so stay on guard. The microphone is always hot. The camera is always on. We **will** ask you questions designed to elicit emotion. It makes for good TV and radio. It works for us. Plus, it is our job. It's what we do.

Chapter 20

"NO COMMENT" - THE KISS OF DEATH

POINT:

If you haven't guessed by now, we are strong proponents of creating a media policy which instructs the media spokesperson(s) to never use "No Comment" as a response to a media inquiry. Most experts on media relations would agree that any comment (perhaps just a "buying time" comment) is far superior to the policy of saying nothing. When you use "No Comment" as your comment, you should fully understand **nothing does not equal zero - it equals less than zero.** You, at that point, are in the hole. You've just made the reporter mad and you've instantly raised suspicion about your credibility. You do not have to start from this position of defensiveness and stepping all over yourself if you use your head.

If there are, in fact, media death wishes, "No Comment" is indeed the kiss of death. After uttering such nonsense, go back to your office and sharpen up those hara-kiri knives, get out the cyanide pills, pull out the silver bullet, and grab the box of straight edge razor blades because you are flirting with committing career and/or corporate suicide.

If you don't believe this, just use your own gut feeling as a gauge on how you feel when observing the news. The next time you see someone use "No Comment" as their statement, stop a couple of seconds and mull over exactly what you thought about them and the company they represent. Will you buy "XYZ" product if the spokesperson won't talk to you about their product? You may not, others may not, in fact, and hundreds of thousands may not. Just remember the Firestone's lack of response to the tire failure on the Ford Explorer if you want further proof.

Yet many companies choose to hold dear the concept "No Comment" is better than commenting primarily for two reasons:

1. They have had a bad experience in the past with the media and it has molded (or tainted) their thinking into the mindset of: "We won't let that happen again." The "If we don't talk, they can't mess with us again." attitude prevails.

2. They have received legal advice about what they say can be used against them in a court of law. Well, of course that is correct, it can. This method of media relations is generally about covering one's posterior way before anyone is thinking about litigation.

Let's look at these two trains of thought a little closer. First, if you got burnt <u>and</u> can't get over it, I can understand to some degree. However, the chief executive will have to explain to me why what happened 15 years ago is still applicable today. Most everyone has forgotten whatever it was that happened, and now, does it really matter? How long can you carry a chip on your shoulder?

In the second proposition of the tail (legal advice) wagging the dog (corporate reputation, industry standing, market share, consumer confidence, etc.), is if you make poorly thought out, stupid statements (especially in a crisis situation) then perhaps you get what you deserve. "Whoops! We forgot to train our spokesperson to be prepared and know how to control and (yes I will say) manipulate the media. Corporate message development? Didn't know we had one, much less promote it. Allowing someone else's story to be told as the truth rather than ours can't be a bad thing, can it?"

You actually should be thinking about the backside of this event when the event begins, and that includes possible litigation. But consider this:

- Litigation is usually an argument over points of fact and points of law.

- Spokespersons generally are not attorneys, so they usually do not speak to points of law. "I don't know about that point of law" will suffice.

- Spokespersons should be trained to speak about the facts of a situation, not to speculate and articulate about the "why" or the cause of an event.

- On the surface at least, the courts, the media, and the media spokesperson all deal in the same world of facts. The "same sheet of music" idea.

- If the spokesperson can master the interview and press conference techniques to relay only the facts as they know them with a sprinkling of factual corporate messaging, you can present in court all the video, audio, and newspapers you want and it should be describing the same set of circumstances.

- If this premise is anywhere close to being accurate, then what harm does it do to present those facts early on in an event (to a reporter) via a corporate spokesperson? Albeit there will be additional "facts" that will emerge by the time the event reaches litigation. (Discovery, etc.)

I am not saying that you do not need to be careful about what you say. The damage done in the marketplace by not

179

commenting needs to be weighed against the perceived advantage it gives you in a courtroom. That is why time must be spent assuring the media policy you draft actually delivers what you want it to accomplish in terms of customer service, satisfaction, and trust.

You may well decide that a strict or modified "No Comment" policy works best. Perhaps you are a decision-maker and the title of this book perked your interest in determining what might be the best policy at your workplace? The final decision is yours, but the majority of evidence points to the conclusion that "No Comment" is not the successful way to engage the media.

Now I have to backpedal just a bit, putting the security consultant's hat on to consider what I just said. The COUNTERPOINT guy will likely disagree with me, but there are a few instances where the "No Comment" philosophy is on target, and a spokesperson can give a kinder, gentler version of saying "No Comment" without the fallout. But these instances are few in number and generally fall under two broad categories:

1. You <u>cannot</u> comment on some public, personnel, and other business records when Federal, State, or Local statute protects them from release. (Most are Federal and are generally personnel or criminal records that pertain to individuals.)

2. Corporate information that is considered proprietary or a trade secret (i.e.; Coca-Cola is not going to give away the secret ingredients to Coke) Reporters may adamantly disagree with that assessment - wanting it because they are the reporters whether it adds any value to their story.

If your situation or crisis has the trappings of the two types of information listed above you can't give up the information under penalty of law. But rather than just saying, "NO COMMENT," you might want to say something like: "I'm sorry I cannot (or am not authorized to) release that information to you because . . . (state your **valid** reason)." You have softened the more offensive, in your face, "No Comment" by stating that you can't release and then explaining the reason why you can't. What happens next can be humorous. First, the reporter looks rather perplexed (more so than normal). Then you can almost see the light bulb go on as they realize you may be withholding information. Usually they don't know the specifics of the law you may be quoting. (Make sure you do.) So they will say nothing, because they don't want to show their peers that they don't know the law. Or they will challenge you about not giving them what they believe is rightfully theirs.

In either case, if you are sure of what you are doing, the ball is now in their court and you have escaped the interview without being scalded with the boiling media witches brew.

If reporters persist, suggest that you continue the discourse in private after the press conference or interview. Then do just that. A little sidebar after the interview shows that you care about their story and you know your stuff well enough to engage in the debate of release of information with them.

You **REALLY** need to assure yourself that the position of non-release is the correct one. Your human resources department or legal counsel can guide you on the statutes and regulations which govern these issues better than I can, so I won't go any further. Stand firm if you know you are right. If the reporter won't budge either, tell them that they may pursue their questions by filing with the courts a "Freedom of Information" (FOI) petition. They likely won't do so unless the issue is one they feel is just too important, or they want to harass you for some reason. Know that if the courts say there is no legal reason for you to withhold the information, you will have to eventually provide it. That is why I suggest that you are relatively sure of your position from the outset. If not, the score at the end of the day is Reporter: 1, Spokesperson: 0.

I'm sure you noticed the POINT guy (that would be me) never has had the last word in any chapter. That's OK because we do want you to see both sides of the coin. (The shiny side and the dark side.) But there is common ground in what I've stated and what you will read in the next few pages. We are in agreement that "No Comment" is the kiss of death. We are so in agreement (unlike us) we purchased the domain name which expresses exactly our views on the subject - www.nocommentsucks.com. Check it out. You'll learn more about the Media Crisis Gurus and how we're helping people get past the fear they have of the evil empire we know as the media.

COUNTERPOINT:

Boy, do we of the evil empire love "No Comment." It's even more fun than a speculating spokesperson. "No Comment" is a free pass to raise all sorts of issues and to interview your competition about you, in depth. To investigate and report everything wrong your organization has ever done and every mistake you've ever made. To talk to every disgruntled employee you've ever had. Anything you've tried to hide (like the reason you felt you needed to go with the "No Comment" strategy in the first place) will come out, be reexamined, and regurgitated in the media.

To the media, "No Comment" says one of two things:

1. Either you are so arrogant that we really need to take you down a peg or two, or

2. You are so naive/stupid that you deserve what you are going to get.

Now you may just be misguided, but the perception of arrogance or incompetence is the reality. "No Comment" is the red flag to the bull, the bloody goat to the piranha, the surfer to the shark.

"No Comment" is a challenge. You are calling us out. It's "The Gunfight at the OK Corral," and believe me, you aren't Wyatt Earp. You may have guns, but we've also got bullets. Fight the media at your peril. You won't win. Trust me.

As we've noted in previous chapters, you do not have to give away proprietary information. Tell us it is proprietary and in most cases we will move on. You've explained to the general public and us why you can't disclose certain information and you've done so in a non-confrontational manner. Normally, we can live with this, unless the "proprietary card" you are playing is a blatant, obvious bluff. Being devious with alleged proprietary information can kill your credibility as well. Play this card only when you are certain the information truly is protected and not just an excuse to duck a hard question. Your manager may not want to see it this way, but you've learned enough from this book to explain the consequences of being untruthful with the media.

Using the "On advice of counsel, I can't comment." card is almost always a bad play too. What are you thinking by listening to an attorney in the first place? Let's face it, their first and foremost reason for existence is CYA. Saying anything might be used in a court of law but, as Ron says, to what effect? If you, as spokesperson, are properly trained and prepared there is very little chance you will say anything remotely litigious. "No Comment" may make sense to your attorney but, in the court of public opinion (your arena); you've just lost the case.

Ok, I was being slightly fatuous about listening to your attorney, but only slightly. They are not trained in marketing and PR, nor are they media experts (though some like to think they are). If you've gotten this far in this book, you've learned a number of strategies on media management. You know that preparation and practice, using the tools we've provided in these chapters, will enable you to face the media, answer their questions effectively, and move on.

As Ron mentioned, he as the CEO, the POINT guy, never gets the last word in this book. Me, the COUNTERPOINT media guy, always gets the last word. So it is in real life. The media **always** gets the last word. You may not like it, but it is reality. Any relationship you develop with the media must be based on that fundamental fact.

By using what you've learned in this book, as well as our CDs, seminars, and consulting services, you can effectively manage/manipulate the media to help ensure that the last word about you is favorable. Ignore our advice and counsel, let your ego get in the way, and the last word about you might be that you're seeking a new place of employment. Is that the last word you want to hear?

ORDER SHEET

Product	Price	Qty.	Subtotal
THE 60 MINUTE MEDIA MANAGER Learn to Plan, Survive and Thrive From Media Experts (60 Minutes)	14.95	_____	_____
THE EMERGENCY URGENCY DRILL How to Best Handle the Media in the 1st 30 Minutes of Any Crisis (30 minutes)	14.95	_____	_____
WHAT DO YOU SAY WHEN YOU *CAN'T SAY ANYTHING* Proven Tips to Get You Past "No Comment" (50 Minutes)	14.95	_____	_____

MANAGING THE MEDIA IN TIMES OF CRISIS - -CALL FOR PRICING AND
On Site Seminar by the Gurus - The Ultimate   AVAILABILITY - -
Learning Experience - Content Rich, Battle Tested -
2 Hrs. to 2 Days - Practical, Insider Media Information

Please *Circle* Your Choices

Package A: Any 2 Audio CD's from the list above (your choice) . $24.95

Package B: All 3 of the Audio CD's from the list above (2 ½ hrs) $35.95

Package C: All 3 of the Audio CD's plus 30 minutes phone
                consulting time with one of the Gurus. $99.95

TOTAL: Please add $5 per item or package for shipping $_____

Guarantee: Don't like it, send it back, and we'll refund the purchase price.

(Please Print)

Name: _____Company: _____

Shipping Address: _____City:_____

State: ____ Zip: _____Phone:_____ Email: _____

Please Send This Form and Check or Money Order To:
The Palmer / McCarthy Group
5147 S. Harvard Ave. #163
Tulsa, Ok. 74135   918-853-4618 or 918-492-5479 - Fax: 918-492-7899

For Credit Card Payment - Use Web Site Shopping Cart (click "Products")
www.mediacrisisgurus.com

ORDER SHEET

Product	Price	Qty.	Subtotal
THE 60 MINUTE MEDIA MANAGER Learn to Plan, Survive and Thrive From Media Experts (60 Minutes)	14.95	____	_____
THE EMERGENCY URGENCY DRILL How to Best Handle the Media in the 1st 30 Minutes of Any Crisis (30 minutes)	14.95	____	_____
WHAT DO YOU SAY WHEN YOU *CAN'T SAY ANYTHING* Proven Tips to Get You Past "No Comment" (50 Minutes)	14.95	____	_____

MANAGING THE MEDIA IN TIMES OF CRISIS　- -CALL FOR PRICING AND
On Site Seminar by the Gurus - The Ultimate　　　　AVAILABILITY - -
Learning Experience - Content Rich, Battle Tested -
2 Hrs. to 2 Days - Practical, Insider Media Information

Please *Circle* Your Choices

Package A: Any 2 Audio CD's from the list above (your choice)　　$24.95

Package B: All 3 of the Audio CD's from the list above (2 ½ hrs)　　$35.95

Package C: All 3 of the Audio CD's plus 30 minutes phone
　　　　　　consulting time with one of the Gurus.　　　　$99.95

TOTAL: Please add $5 per item or package for shipping　　　$_____

Guarantee: Don't like it, send it back, and we'll refund the purchase price.

(Please Print)

Name: _____Company: _____

Shipping Address: _____City:_____

State: ___ Zip: _____Phone:_____ Email: _____

Please Send This Form and Check or Money Order To:
The Palmer / McCarthy Group
5147 S. Harvard Ave. #163
Tulsa, Ok. 74135　　918-853-4618 or 918-492-5479 - Fax: 918-492-7899

For Credit Card Payment - Use Web Site Shopping Cart (click "Products")
www.mediacrisisgurus.com